james lincoln collier

inside

jazz

four winds press
new york

Books on music by James Lincoln Collier
  Which Musical Instrument Shall I Play?
  Practical Music Theory
  Jug Bands and Homemade Music

Also by the same author
  The Teddy Bear Habit
  Rock Star (Winner of the 1970 Award,
              Children's Book Committee,
              Child Study Association)

2   3   4   5   6   78 77 76 75 74

Published by Four Winds Press.
A Division of Scholastic Magazines, Inc., New York, N.Y.
Copyright © 1973 by James Lincoln Collier.
All rights reserved.
Printed in the United States of America.
Library of Congress Catalogue Card Number: 73–76455
Printed in the U.S.A.

for justine,
john & eliza

acknowledgments

I'D LIKE TO THANK THE NUMBERLESS JAZZ MUSICIANS, scholars, and jazz enthusiasts with whom, over the years, I have warmly argued many of the points in this book. More specifically, record collectors William A. Robbins, William H. Dunham, Lee Lorenz, and Robert Andrew Parker made valuable suggestions for the discography listed at the end of the book. Finally, my particular thanks to Dr. John L. Fell, specialist in popular culture at San Francisco State College, for reading the manuscript and saving me from a number of errors both of omission and commission. Needless to say, the opinions herein are my own.

contents

In later years the great Louis Armstrong worked mostly with a Dixieland band which featured his singing more than his trumpet playing. Here he is shown with the brilliant trombonist Jack Teagarden, who played with the Armstrong band in the 1950s. (CULVER PICTURES)

a jazz lover's story

I EARN MY LIVING AS A PROFESSIONAL WRITER. BUT ever since I played in my first jam session at the age of fourteen, I have always been at least a part-time jazz musician, too. Jazz is not the only kind of music I enjoy; I also like playing music by Bach and Beethoven. But jazz is my first love, the music I am utterly at home with, the music I consider my friend when I need one. That first jam session when I was fourteen occurred during lunch hour in the high-school band room; while going to my first afternoon class, carrying my still uneaten lunch, I was shaken and ecstatic to think that I, *me*, had actually played some jazz. I can't say I am always quite so ecstatic about a jam session today, but playing jazz still gives me a thrill.

I am not alone. I have played jazz in night clubs, concert halls, and private jam sessions all across the United States and Europe, from San Francisco to New York, from London to Leningrad, and I can tell you that across the face of the earth there are millions of people who are as devoted to this particular kind of music as I am.

Jazz is a brand new music, newer by far than symphonic music, opera, or most kinds of folk music. It is, in fact, not much older than the span of one man's life. The great trumpet player Louis Armstrong was born in 1900, when jazz was hardly out of the cradle, and he died in 1971. Sixty years ago jazz was virtually unknown outside the black ghettos of New Orleans and a few other places in the South. Today it is one of the most important musical forms played anywhere. Why this particular music spread so far and so fast is difficult to say; it is not easy to understand why one kind of music grips people more than another. In any case, it is certainly obvious that jazz, for whatever reason, has a deep and real meaning for many people of all nationalities and races.

I am willing to go further, in fact, and say that jazz is the most important music being played in the Western world today. It is not necessarily the most popular; at the present time rock music is. Nor is it necessarily "the best" music. Everybody has his own idea of what "the best" music is. Young people today generally prefer rock, and certainly so-called "classical music" is much richer and more varied in many respects than jazz. Nevertheless, I insist that jazz is the most important of them all, because at the present time it is acting as the source, or feeding stream, for much of the other music now being created. Rock, folk music, popular songs, the theme music of movies and television shows, even march music, country music, and much modern classical music is heavily indebted to jazz. The jazz influence is everywhere. Indeed, rock could hardly have come into being without the jazz background.

Of course, not everybody cares for jazz. It has never really been a "popular" music in the way that big band swing of the 1930s, rock of the 1960s, or the music of famous singers like Frank Sinatra or Dionne Warwick have been popular. The rock groups and the swing band leaders became celebrities, and their records sold in the millions. Few jazz records have ever sold that many, and the only jazz players who have become celebrities are ones like Louis Armstrong, who was famous not for his jazz solos, but for singing popular songs. People don't realize that he was possibly the greatest jazz musician who ever lived.

So jazz has never appealed to everyone. But those who are attracted to it are likely to end up caring for it deeply —so deeply that it becomes an important part of their lives. I don't mean just the musicians who play it, either. There are millions of jazz fans around the world who would rather listen to jazz than do anything else. They play their favorite records over and over; they listen to the music several hours a day; they travel hundreds of miles to hear musicians they especially admire.

Because jazz is so well liked by so many people, it is not at all surprising that it should be influential. This does not mean, of course, that rock, folk, and other types of music stemmed directly from jazz. The story is a bit more complicated and it begins with the idea that jazz is not so much a "type" of music but *a way of playing music*.

This is a very important point. Although jazz players prefer to work with certain types of songs, there are no jazz songs as such: virtually any song can be played as jazz. In the hands of a good jazz musician even a simple tune like "Happy Birthday to You" can become jazz. On the other hand, a musician without an understanding of jazz can play a standard jazz song like "St. Louis Blues" and it will not be jazz.

Now, because jazz is not a kind of music, but a way of playing music, you can see how it could influence other types of music—why it has been so profoundly influential throughout the entire world. (Jazz is much more important in Europe and North America than it is in Africa and Asia, but there is a great deal of interest in jazz in countries like Japan and Thailand as well.) Because so many composers, arrangers, and performers like jazz, it keeps creeping into music everywhere. Thus, no matter what kind of contemporary music a person prefers, jazz is likely to be a part of it.

But the way jazz influences other music is not a simple thing. Rock, for instance, has always been heavily affected by jazz and indeed continues to be. Rock did not stem directly from jazz. It grew out of a combination of various types of popular music that existed in the 1950s. One of these was the blues. I'll discuss the blues in more detail later in this book, but let me say for the moment that the blues, essentially, is kin to jazz. Another type of music that went into making rock was what is called "rhythm and blues"—a sort of popularization of jazz much in favor in the 1940s and 1950s among black people in the big cities. Another element that went into rock was country music. Country music has never been highly influenced by jazz, but jazz has had a moderate effect on it. So, while rock did not grow directly out of jazz, it grew out of forms of music which were involved with the jazz tradition. Rock musicians of course combined these types into something new and different and quite fascinating, and inevitably, a lot of jazz feeling got into the new music.

Because jazz has influenced so much of the music we hear around us, it is worth knowing something about. First, we will need answers to some important questions: What is jazz? In what ways is it different from other music? Where did it come from? What is it like?

John Gillespie acquired the nickname "Dizzy" for his
hi-jinks on the bandstand, but there is nothing comical about
his bravura solo work built on dazzling technical skills.
(CULVER PICTURES)

2

what is jazz?

JAZZ HAS MANY SPECIAL CHARACTERISTICS BUT THERE
are two of supreme importance—so important in fact that
if they aren't present you don't have jazz. One is a certain
feeling that we can only call the jazz rhythm; the second
is the fact that jazz basically is always improvised.

Let's begin by talking about rhythm. It is a very difficult subject because, like many other aspects of music, it
is much easier to understand by hearing than by talking
about it. But talking helps.

All music can be broken down into three components:
form, harmony, and rhythm. The form of a piece is its
shape. How many sections is it divided into? Are they of
equal length or are some longer? Are some parts repeated? Is the whole piece long or short? There are only
a handful of jazz forms and, by classical standards anyway, they are ludicrously simple—although to be fair, a

few modern jazz players have experimented with slightly more complex forms.

Harmony is the word we use to talk about which notes can be played together and how they can be combined. Harmonically, jazz is not very different from other music. There are differences, of course, especially in the so-called "blue notes," which fall in between certain other notes, as if in between the keys on the piano. (I'll discuss blue notes in more detail in a later chapter.) But the ways in which jazz musicians combine notes to make up melodies and chords are similar to the ways in which it is done in folk music, classical music, and much of the rest of our music. Beethoven would have no trouble understanding most jazz harmonies.

That leaves rhythm, and here is the crucial distinction between jazz and all other music. You can make rhythm by banging a drum with a drumstick—or a pot with a spoon, for that matter. But that isn't the only way rhythm is made. In music most rhythm is created by the notes themselves—in how fast they come along, how short ones are combined with long ones, and where they happen to begin and end. The beat of every song is virtually locked into the melody.

In jazz, a drum or some other instrument usually states the basic beat. But far more important is the special type of jazz rhythm locked into the musical phrases played by the various instruments. This particular rhythmic feel is the heart, the soul, the life of jazz. Anybody who knows even a little about it can recognize jazz when he hears it by the rhythm alone. Take, for example, a trumpet solo by Louis Armstrong. If you leave the notes the same, but change their length and their spacing even slightly, you can take all the jazz out of it. Now do it the other way around—change the notes but leave their rhythm the same. You will still have jazz, although perhaps not as interesting a solo as the one Armstrong played. As a matter of fact, you can remove the notes from a good jazz solo altogether and simply tap it out on a table with a pencil and the jazz feeling will remain.

What exactly is this jazz rhythm? One of its characteristics is what is called syncopation. Most music has a basic beat that you can tap your foot to, and generally those beats are organized into blocks or groups we call measures. Waltzes, for instance, are usually organized into blocks of three beats to a measure, marches with two beats to a measure, and so forth. Jazz is usually played four beats to a measure (although players today are experimenting with other beat patterns, or time signatures as they are usually called) but that isn't the main point. In jazz, very often the notes don't come on the beat. They come *in between* the beats, perhaps carrying over across to the next one. They may even carry over across into the next measure, and end between two beats there. Playing between the beats is called syncopation. There is plenty of syncopation in other kinds of music: Bach, for example, used many syncopated figures in his fugues and inventions. But jazz is so riddled with syncopation that hardly a measure goes by without it. Of course, not every jazz note is syncopated. I have just checked over a short solo by Louis Armstrong: out of forty-four notes, nineteen are syncopated, and there is at least one syncopated figure in eight of the nine measures.

Syncopation, then, is a crucial characteristic of jazz. But there is more to the subject of jazz rhythm than syncopation, and here is where words stop being useful. Jazz players do things with rhythms which are very subtle, which cannot be really written down on paper, but which nonetheless can be felt. For one thing, players often begin their notes just slightly ahead or behind the beat. By this I don't mean the syncopated notes. Even the notes that are supposedly played right on the beat are often slightly ahead or behind. Armstrong, to use him as an example again, characteristically hit his notes just slightly late of where a strict player would have put them.

Secondly, jazz players usually have their own personal ways of dividing up a sequence of notes. For instance, in other types of music, a series of notes probably will be given equal length, like this:

——— ——— ——— ——— ———

Or they may be divided into markedly unequal lengths, like this:

——— —— ——— —— ———

Jazz players, on the other hand, are likely to play that same sequence of notes so that the short ones are only slightly shorter than the long ones, like this:

——— —— ——— —— ———

The difference is subtle but it is quite real and is virtually impossible to write down in ordinary musical notation. Furthermore, no two jazz players do it exactly the same way. Dizzy Gillespie, the great bop trumpet player, has a tendency to play the notes in his fast runs virtually equally, while Coleman Hawkins, the tenor saxophone master, characteristically plays the first note of a pair about half again as long as the second. (Although it is interesting to note that Hawkins plays the notes more equally when he is going up than when he is coming down.)

Then there is the question of accent. Even where notes are given equal length, one may be played sharper or louder than another. Hawkins, again, sometimes accents the long notes in a run so much that the short notes are almost swallowed up. In fact, in much jazz playing there are notes which almost don't exist. You feel their presence more than you hear them; you know they're supposed to be there even though they're virtually inaudible. Hawkins plays many of these invisible notes.

Finally, there is the fact that most jazz is played legato. Staccato notes are notes which are sharply separated from each other. Legato notes are joined, each one being held over until the next one starts. Of course, staccato playing also exists in jazz. But legato playing far and away predominates; and this again means that the rhythms implied by the soloist are somewhat blurred.

On the whole, then, given all these devices, you can see that jazz melodies tend to slip and slide over the underlying beat, instead of being firmly locked into it, as in many other types of music. It is like a boy watching out for the cracks on the sidewalk: most types of music step firmly on the cracks, or equally firmly avoid them: jazz just runs helter-skelter, ignoring the cracks altogether. This contrast between the basic beat and the rhythmic figures being improvised by the jazz player is the most crucial single aspect of jazz. And of course it helps to explain why jazz bands invariably have some sort of rhythm section—that is a drum or bass or combination of instruments more or less marking out the time. Because so much of the meaning of jazz lies in the way the melody slips and slides around the basic beat, it is important to establish the beat, so that the contrast can be made.

Thus, jazz is not so much which notes are being played but the way they are played to create a certain rhythmic feel. This feeling is usually covered by the word "swing" but nobody has ever adequately defined the word swing. (Furthermore, the term is also used for the big "swing" bands of the 1930s and 1940s—some of which didn't swing very much.) We can say, however, that jazz rhythm is propulsive. It seems to go rushing along, endlessly pushing forward as if determined to get somewhere, at the same time holding the listener in a kind of suspense. It is a little like a mountain stream; the water rushes headlong by, yet as it passes in front of an observer, it bubbles and curls in constantly changing patterns.

Because rhythm is so crucial to jazz, we should not think that harmonies and melodies don't matter. They do matter a great deal. There are plenty of solos played every day which use perfectly good jazz rhythms but which still are dull or even just plain awful because the player used meaningless or bad melodic figures. Any jazz musician can play at least reasonably good jazz rhythms or he wouldn't be considered a jazz musician; but the great players make not only fascinating rhythms but lovely and sometimes astonishing melodic inventions, too. Nonetheless, the fact remains that you can play jazz without melody, but music without the characteristic rhythms cannot be called jazz. Once you catch the feeling of jazz rhythm and can tap out a jazz beat with a pencil, you have learned what the music is basically all about.

This brings us to the second important characteristic of jazz, improvisation. Improvisation means to make something up on the spur of the moment. Basically all jazz is improvised, and this holds true even though it is sometimes written down. This contradiction is explained by the fact that you can't really write down jazz in the way that you can write down other kinds of music. All its rhythmic subtleties simply defy notation. The music a jazz player reads is only a kind of guideline; the player must add those rhythmic subtleties himself—he must "improvise" them. If you had ever played in a big jazz band you would understand how true this is. In a marching band, for example, when all the players read the music properly it all comes out the same. But because every jazz player interprets the music in his own way, adding subtle accents according to his own style and feeling, every member of a jazz group reads a score differently. In a big jazz band, therefore, each section has a leader—the first trumpet player or the first alto saxophone player—whom everybody else in the section follows in this matter of accents and rhythms—what jazz players call "phrasing."

But in any case most jazz is not written down; it is entirely improvised. This is something many listeners find mystifying. Are they really making it up as they go along? How can they do that and make it sound right? How do they know what the other players are going to do? What is going on in a musician's head when he improvises?

Of course, jazz is not the only music that is improvised. As a matter of fact, most kinds of music all over the world are at least partly improvised. As a music maker, man is an improviser. The European system, in which the music is all written down exactly, is really the unusual way, not the standard. Actually, even in Europe, music was not entirely written down until about two hundred years ago. In Baroque keyboard music, for example, quite often the composer merely suggested a harmonic outline for the bass, leaving the exact notes to be worked out by the player.

Then too, all European music is not the formal music of symphonies and concertos. Folk or popular music has always existed as well. Although this popular music was not purely improvised, it seems probable that the musicians took liberties with the tunes, changing them around a bit from time to time as it suited them. And because they were not written down, no doubt they changed over the years as different musicians played them in different ways.

In general it is safe to say that most of the music made by man is improvised. But musicians do not simply improvise out of thin air: they always work within some kind of a framework. Improvising is a bit like talking on a given subject. Suppose somebody says to you, "Tell me what your school is like." You don't read something you've written down, you "make it up as you go along," and you are therefore improvising. Nonetheless, you can't just throw out any combination of words that comes into your head: you speak within a framework. Of course, one person might have trouble thinking of things to say and stammer over his words, while another might have funny or interesting things to tell on the subject; but both are improvising.

So do musicians improvise. It may be a melody which the player varies to suit himself. It may be, as with much African music, a set of rhythms against which the players improvise other rhythms. It may be a blues melody twisted about to suit the words and the feelings of the singer. It may be a Baroque trumpet embellishment to the melody line.

Thus, the jazz musician is not unique but is following

in a long musical tradition. Like the rest, he works within a framework. It is interesting to note that one of the things that distinguishes the major jazz styles from each other is that their frameworks are slightly different. The modern soloist is thinking about something different from the New Orleans player when he improvises.

In the earliest New Orleans jazz, played by bands which evolved out of parade bands, there was not much true improvisation. According to one player who worked with these bands, the musicians were really "embellishers," who dressed up the melody lines with little decorative figures and accents. Each of the players—the clarinet, cornet, and trombones—had a melodic line memorized which he stuck to more or less, although of course he would play it with a jazz-accented rhythm. But as jazz began to develop and jazz musicians began to learn more about reading music and musical theory, a new framework for improvising gradually came into use. This framework, this new approach, has remained the basis of jazz improvisation up to the present time, although at this moment the free jazz style is offering yet another approach.

The durable framework on which jazz improvisation has been built for the past fifty years is the chord progression, referred to by musicians as "the changes." Those who know something about music will understand what a chord is, and will realize that a chord progression is a string of chords laid out in a row. For those who don't understand music, the best explanation is to say that a chord progression is the harmony which underlies a song or any piece of music. This harmony shifts and changes as the song progresses. Every song has its chord progression or underlying harmony and so, of course, does the blues, which is fundamentally a chord progression without any preset melody to underlie. For example, at a given point in a song the melody might be on the notes C and A. Now, there are a number of harmonies, or chords, which will fit in with those notes. In the ordinary song played by a jazz musician, one specific chord has been chosen by the composer, the arranger, or the musicians themselves to go with those notes at that place. (In a different part of the song a different chord might be set to the same notes.) When the jazz player improvises, he tries to think of something to play which will fit in with that harmony. Ordinarily that means emphasizing some of the notes which are actually in that chord. For example, suppose an A minor chord is called for. The player knows that an A minor chord contains the notes A, C, and E, and he will tend to emphasize one or all of those notes at this point.

But which notes does he emphasize, and why? There, of course, is where training and creative skills come in. The really fine jazz musician actually hears in his head what he will play next before he comes to it. All he has to do then is play what he hears—something nearly anyone can learn to do with practice. Charlie Parker said that he was able to hear what he was going to play several bars in advance—so far in advance, he claimed, that he might change it in his head before he actually caught up to it. Most players probably don't hear more than a few notes in advance, however. Other players don't hear very far ahead at all, and rely a great deal on their knowledge of music to help them along. That is to say, the very fact that an A minor chord followed by a D^7 chord are to be played at a certain point suggests to the knowledgeable player certain notes to play. Both of those chords contain the notes C and A; obviously, one thing the improviser might do at that point in the tune is to build a little bit of melody around those two notes.

What kind of melody is another question. Generally speaking, in jazz improvisation which notes you choose are less important than the way you choose to play them. This follows from a point I made earlier, that it is not the notes but the rhythms which characterize jazz—making it distinctly its own type of music. Many very fine jazz solos, if reduced to their notes alone, prove to be exceedingly simple: it is the way the notes are played, especially the rhythmic pattern in which they are played, that matters.

These things often can be very subtle—a matter of a slight accent here or there, as I have said. Sometimes it is a question of holding a note out a little longer than the listener expects, or jumping in with the next note early, or playing the notes just a fraction ahead of the beat or a bit behind. Then there is the whole matter of which notes to emphasize, which notes to slide over lightly. And of course most jazz players have a variety of tone colors they can use—perhaps a bit of roughness they can add to certain notes for emphasis or variety.

Choosing how to play the notes is something that can't be taught. Either the musician develops a feel for it or he doesn't—and if he doesn't, he isn't a jazz player. Of course nobody is born with this feel for jazz. It is learned simply by hearing the music a lot. Most of the great jazz players grew up with it all around them from childhood; it was practically in the air they breathed. Louis Armstrong, for example, talked about hearing jazz, even then

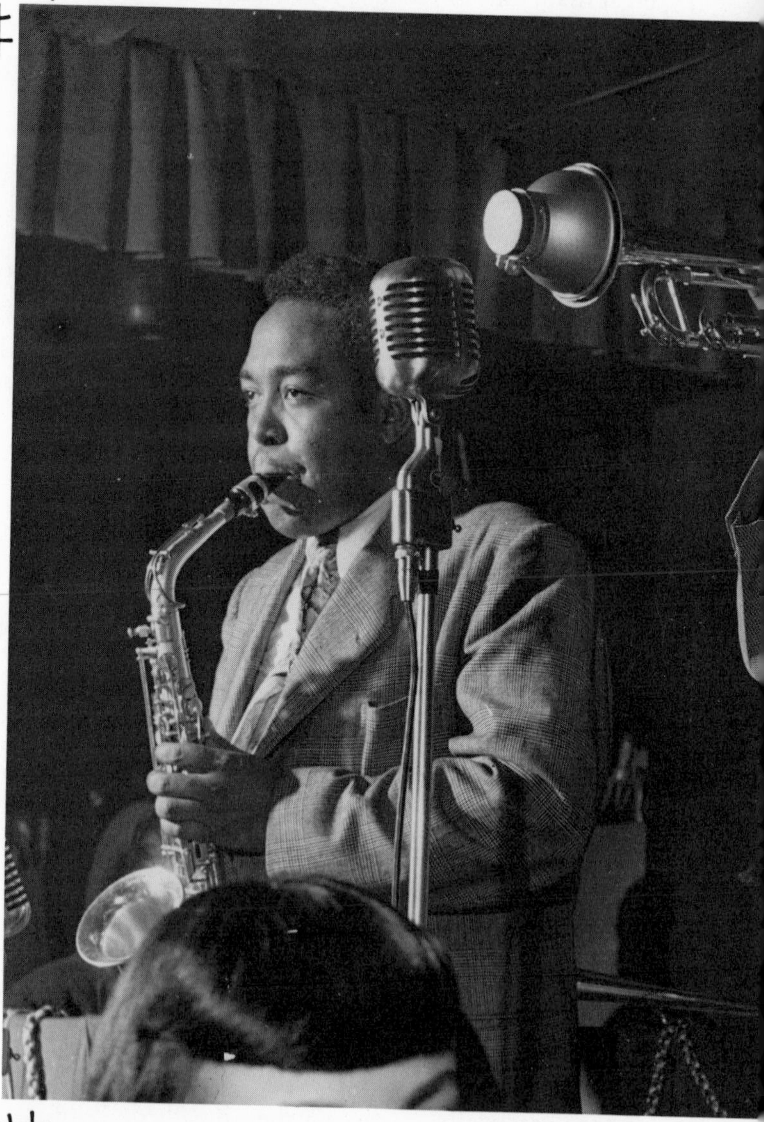

After Armstrong, Charlie "Bird" Parker is generally considered to have been the greatest of all jazz improvisers. As Armstrong had done earlier, Parker in the 1940s reshaped the whole nature of the music. His influence is still important today. With him in this picture taken in 1949 is trumpeter Kenny Dorham. (CULVER PICTURES)

brand new, from his earliest youth in the streets of New Orleans.

And this explains why so many blacks become good jazz musicians. More than white children, black ghetto children hear jazz, or at least jazz-influenced music like rhythm-and-blues or so-called "soul music," practically from birth. White families are more likely to have popular music or even classical music on the radio or record player than they are music with jazz inflections. The child from the black ghetto hears his jazz around him all the time, blaring from the record shops, from apartment windows, in barber shops and stores.

Developing a feel for jazz rhythms, accents, and inflections, then, is something that you do simply by listening to a lot of jazz. Learning what notes to play, however, is something that you can pick up from a book. If you have an interest in learning how to improvise jazz, the best thing to do is to study a little music theory. You don't need to learn very much, just enough to get the idea of what chords are, how they are put together in a progression, and what melody notes go along with which chords. You can learn this in a few weeks if you are willing to do a bit of studying.*

In the early days of jazz the players knew very little about chords, harmonies, and music theory, which is one reason why they improvised only within very strict limits. When playing the blues, for example, they knew a certain set of notes which "worked," and they stuck to them without wandering too far afield. But most jazz players today are thoroughly trained musicians. They not only are ex-

---

* The author's "Practical Music Theory" is a useful guide for the beginning musician.

ceedingly expert on their instruments but usually have studied composition as well as basic theory. They know enough so that figuring out what notes to play at any given moment is almost second nature to them. When they improvise, they usually do not consciously work out harmonies in their heads; instead, they *listen*.

Listening is a very important part of jazz playing. A musician who is improvising is not playing by himself, after all; there are other players working with him. The saxophone player not only hears what the trumpet player is doing, he is probably paying special attention to the line being laid down by the string bass. Sometimes it is the piano player who "lays down chords" for the other players. Each jazz musician has his own special things he listens for when he is improvising. In a sense, a good jazz musician can improvise on a song he has never heard before, simply by listening to the notes and chords being played by the piano or bass or whatever instrument is laying down the basic line. There are, of course, limits to what anybody can hear; much depends on training. The novice jazz player may be able to hear one chord following another, but he may not be sure exactly what notes are in the chords. The experienced player usually knows fairly well what is being played around him most of the time, unless it is something quite complicated or unfamiliar to him.

Today, hearing what is going on around him is more important than ever to the jazz improviser. "New thing" or free jazz often does without chord changes all together: the players are allowed to go in almost any direction, without regard for the traditional rules of musical theory. But this does not mean the musician is totally unrestricted in what he plays. The crucial thing is for him to listen carefully to the other players, in order to fit in with them. Because he has fewer harmonic rules to guide him, listening is more important to him than to the Dixieland musician, for example, who can play an acceptable solo just by following the rules even if he can't hear the rest of the band at all.

What the musician hears being played by the other musicians of course suggests to him things to play himself. In the end he is *thinking musically*. He is not thinking, "This is a Bb chord coming up, so I can play a D or an F to fit into it." Instead there are sounds pouring into his head from outside; these sounds suggest other sounds which his head is sorting out. He does not put it into words—there isn't time for that. He is listening to sounds from outside and from inside. He is thinking *musically*. To give an example: visualize in your mind a cube. Now turn that cube into something else. You are thinking *visually*. An artist doesn't say to himself, "Oh yes, a square here will relate nicely to that circle there"; instead, he sees in his head how shapes might fit together and puts them down. He thinks visually and draws. The jazz player thinks musically and plays.

This makes it sound as if the music pours out automatically, and to an extent it does. The musician is not thinking about what keys or valves to push to get the sound he wants: long years of training have made that happen for him automatically. But the truth is, no jazz musician is a perfect improviser. Sometimes no very interesting ideas come up and he falls back on something he has played before, even an old tired cliché. Sometimes when his ideas are not flowing very well he falls back on theory to give him something to work with. Sometimes he mishears what is going on, sometimes he plays a figure awkwardly, sometimes he just plain gets mixed up and the wrong notes come out. All of the greatest jazz musicians have played many dull, jumbled, tasteless solos.

All of this makes it sound as if improvising is very difficult, but in fact it isn't really so hard once you get some practice at it, especially if you know a little music theory. Many, if not most, of the important jazz musicians began by copying ideas and solos from older musicians they admired: it isn't a bad way to begin.

Of course, the great musician brings to his improvising more than the right notes and a feeling for jazz rhythms. He brings a personal quality, his own style, to his music that makes him instantly indentifiable to the knowledgeable listener. Any jazz player or fan will recognize immediately, from just a few notes, the playing of Louis Armstrong or Charlie Parker. These great musicians have qualities which set them apart. Not only are their tones unique; they also bring startling ideas, brilliant musical inventions which avoid the obvious, and a dramatic flow which ties a whole solo together, making it a unit rather than a series of unrelated musical ideas. The truly great jazz musician is great for the same reasons that a great writer or painter is great: he can make a unified whole out of fascinating parts which join in surprising ways. And we can only explain how he does it by saying that he is a genius.

Ferdinand "Jelly Roll" Morton, a flamboyant character, was one of the first musicians to find ways of orchestrating jazz without sacrificing any of its natural color and force. (THE NEW YORK PUBLIC LIBRARY, Astor, Lenox and Tilden Foundations)

3

how it all began

JAZZ WAS CREATED BY AMERICAN BLACKS. IT WAS PUT together by joining elements of the music they brought with them from Africa with the music of the white people who had come from Europe. It is interesting that this most typical American art form is made up of elements developed in the Old World—Africa and Europe, for of course the white music of America was strictly a European product.

Jazz is distinctly not "African" music. Most Africans don't understand it very well because it is so different from their own music. Neither is it "European" music; much of it is totally unlike anything that developed in Germany, France, and Italy over the past thousand years. Sometimes when you mix two things together you get something very different: blue and yellow together make green, which is neither a "bluish" color nor a "yellowish" color but something distinctly new. This is the case with jazz:

although it was built of a combination of African and European music, it is neither, but something special of its own.

Although jazz is not African music, it is, without question, the creation of American blacks. There have been many great white jazz musicians like Jack Teagarden, Benny Goodman, and Stan Getz, three influential players who have made important contributions to the music. The fact remains that these white players were taking up a music which had been created first by blacks. Furthermore, on any list of, say, the top twenty jazz players, probably fifteen would be blacks. The great innovators in jazz, like Louis Armstrong, Duke Ellington, and Charlie Parker, probably the three most influential of all players, are black.

I don't mean, however, that jazz is black man's music. It is *American* music and belongs to all of us, white and black both. Even though it was created by blacks, it is now part of our American heritage. To those of us who have grown up with it, it seems as natural as eating. To be sure, there are some extremely good jazz players in other countries, and no doubt as time goes on and jazz becomes more and more widespread, other nations will produce many more good players. But the truth is that although a few non-Americans play jazz well, most simply can't compare with our American players. Jazz is a musical language that Americans understand better than anyone else. Where, then, did it come from?

The first African slaves were brought to the United States in 1619. They continued to come in a flood for over two hundred more years, and of course they brought with them their own language, traditions, ways of doing things.

One of these traditions was music. For these African peoples music was not merely an entertainment but was woven through their entire lives. According to Eileen Southern, an authority on black music, "Ceremonial music composed the largest part of the musical repertory of a village of a people. Music accompanied religious ceremonies and rites associated with birth, initiation, marriage, healing, going to war, and death. . . . The Ashanti thought it 'absurd' to worship their god in any way other than with chanting or singing." Among some groups, people actually sang or chanted their arguments to the judge when they were involved in a lawsuit. In fact, so closely were Africans involved with music that in some cases notes were actually words that could be understood by the listener. This should not be surprising when we realize that African drums were used as a kind of sound language by which messages could be sent great distances.

Thus, among Africans, music had a great deal more importance in daily life than it does in ours. There are many Americans who "aren't interested" in music. They never make any particular effort to hear any and they wouldn't really miss it if it disappeared entirely. No such people existed among those blacks who were brought here as slaves. It was such an important way of communicating, of expressing themselves, of giving them a feeling of belonging, that they could no more be uninterested in music than they could be uninterested in breathing.

The music of these African peoples was essentially rhythmic. They had, of course, a few rudimentary whistles, flutes, stringed instruments and such, and of course they could sing. But the range of melodies and harmonies they played on these instruments was very limited compared with the kind of music that was being played in Europe during the same time. On the other hand, their rhythms were extraordinarily complex, so complex in fact that Western musicologists still have difficulty unraveling them. To simplify the story a good deal, African music was based on a steady, underlying beat, over which a number of other beats were laid by other musicians. To American ears, these different beats appear to have no relationship to each other; they confuse us. But to the African who has grown up with that kind of music it all makes perfect sense: he can hear how the beats fit together, how it all means something. By Western standards, the accomplishments of African musicians are amazing, so far as rhythm is concerned. Few American musicians could even begin to play some of the rhythms that Africans take for granted. Try tapping out three beats with your hand in the same length of time that you pat four times with your feet. You probably can't do it but African musicians may keep six very different beats going at once.

African music was not just rhythm. Africans sang and played melodies on their relatively simple instruments. In general, these melodies were based on a scale that is something like the ordinary Western "do-re-mi-fa-sol-la-ti-do" scale we all know. There were differences, however, and later on we will see how these differences played a role in the way blues are sung today.

Naturally, when these blacks were brought as slaves to the United States, their interest in music continued. Of course, it was no longer woven through their lives as it had been in Africa, but nevertheless it continued to play an important role.

Although some blacks were treated reasonably well by

their masters, and a few actually managed to become free, most American blacks lived lives of abject misery. Just being a slave is bad enough; but blacks were often beaten for minor infractions of the rules, often did not have enough to eat, and lived in rough huts many times not protected from the weather, and were frequently separated from their families on a slave owner's whim. But above all, the thing that characterized their lives was work. Slaves worked from dawn till dusk, and sometimes later, six days a week. It was the hardest, most grinding, most deadly monotonous kind of work, too: stooping all day in the fields to pick or reap, chopping endless forests of trees, carrying great loads fourteen hours a day on the docks. The black was forced to live for work; it was his life. And inevitably, he put music into his work to ease the misery.

Many people have fitted chants and songs to the rhythm of their work. Think of the sailors singing sea chanteys as they pushed the capstan around to raise an anchor, or the famous "Song of the Volga Boatman" which is supposed to fit to the strokes of the oars. But black slaves, with their strong musical tradition, put songs to any type of work. Eighteenth-century travelers often reported on the chants of the black boatmen as they ferried passengers across rivers. Black stevedores on the docks sang as they toted their heavy loads onto the ships. One stevedore song reported from the Philadelphia area around 1800 went:

Nancy Bohannan, she married a barber,
Shave her away, shave her away;
He shaved all he could, he couldn't shave harder,
Shave her away, shave her away.

There were other songs for wood-cutting, timed to the strokes of the axe, there were songs for husking corn, songs for reaping grain, songs for all of the myriad activities that the slaves were forced to perform.

But work songs were far from the whole of the black's music. In some places, partly out of kindness, but probably more because it was a good way of letting the slaves blow off steam, blacks were often allowed to put on musical festivals much like the ones they had learned at home. The most famous of these were the Sunday festivals in New Orleans in a place called Congo Square, but there were others all over the country, even up into the northern part of New York State. Huge crowds of slaves would gather in a field which had been stamped hard and bare of grass by years of dancing. The musicians would play and the other slaves would dance as they had in Africa, sometimes for hours, often until they dropped exhausted to the ground. These festivals were not necessarily weekly occurrences but might come only once a year and last as long as a week at a time.

The work songs and the festival music were in general very close to the music the blacks had known in Africa. Traditions no doubt changed somewhat but because new blacks were steadily arriving all through the 17th and 18th centuries, those who were born here had an opportunity to learn at first hand their musical heritage. But gradually, black music began to merge with white.

There were two forces mainly responsible for this. One was the fact that in colonial America there was a great demand for musicians, especially fiddlers, who could play dance music. It is hard for us to imagine today, but dancing was one of the most important social functions through the first two hundred and fifty years of America's history. Most people don't realize it, but sports—all that golf, tennis, and basketball which is so much a part of our lives—didn't really exist until a hundred years ago or so. Colonial Americans did not play sports nearly as much as we do. Instead, they used dancing to get the same kind of physical release we find in bowling or tennis. Thus, the demand for musicians who could play the proper dance tunes was high. Inevitably, numbers of blacks put together homemade violins and flutes and learned how to play dance music. Sometimes a master would actually have a slave instructed in music so as to have a dance musician always on hand. For the slaves, music was a way out of the endless drudgery of hoeing, planting, and picking. Far better to play dances for "Massa" than to stoop over his cotton in the broiling sun fourteen hours a day.

Thus was started a tradition of black dance musicians which continued down into the first part of this century. Even as late as World War I it was considered somehow beneath the dignity of a middle-class white child to learn to play dance tunes. It was all right to play hymns or Beethoven sonatas, but not dance tunes. Of course, not all dance musicians were black; but certainly a high percentage of them were. In any case, as the blacks established themselves as dance musicians, it was inevitable that they would carry some white music home to the slave quarters.

A second, and undoubtedly more important influence, was the church. America was founded at least partly on religious principles. In the early days, not belonging to the church was unthinkable. Naturally, the early settlers assumed that black slaves ought to be given the benefits of religion, and to one degree or another the slave owners insisted that the slaves partake of religious ceremonies.

Hymn singing in colonial days and even later was an

important part of religious worship. In some churches the minister would sing a line from a psalm or other religious text and the congregation would sing it back to him. This was known then as "lining out" the hymn; now we refer to this type of music as "call-and-response."

As it happens, this call-and-response pattern was very familiar to the slaves, for a great deal of the African music they had learned at home employed it. Typically a leader would sing or chant the lines of a song, while the others would answer each line with the same response. One such song goes like this:

> Give flesh to the hyenas at daybreak,
>   Oh, the broad spears!
> The spear of the Sultan is the broadest,
>   Oh, the broad spears!
> I behold thee now—I desire to see none other,
>   Oh, the broad spears!
> My horse is as tall as a high wall,
>   Oh, the broad spears!

In this case, the leader probably was improvising his lines as he went along, with the rest simply repeating the line "Oh, the broad spears!" It is possible that one of the reasons for the answering line from the chorus was to give the leader a chance to think up a new line.

Thus, when black slaves were brought into the church this call-and-response pattern was quite familiar to them. They began rapidly to adapt to the white man's music, and when they began forming churches of their own they carried this music along with them.

It should not be thought that blacks had to be forced to go to church. Some did of course; no doubt a great many slaves were indifferent to the white man's God. But for millions of others the Christian church service was a moment of solace and, indeed, pleasure. For a people with a tradition of music in religion as the blacks had, the early American church's heavy emphasis on music must have seemed natural and right.

The exodus of blacks from the white church began around 1800, although there had been a few scattered black churches established earlier. In some instances the blacks were put out of the churches by prejudiced whites, but more often the blacks left of their own accord to escape the role of second-class citizen they played in the churches. The new black churches continued to use the same hymnals in use in the white churches but inevitably they began to add African inflections and rhythms to the hymns as they sang them. So once again, European and African influences were brought together by black people to make a change in American music.

During this same period there occurred in the United States a religious revival movement known as the "Second Awakening" in which an attempt was made to infuse religion with more enthusiasm and fervor. An important development of this movement was the so-called "camp meeting." A camp meeting was a gathering of hundreds, perhaps thousands, of worshippers to a specially erected tent city. Preaching went on day and night and very often it was of the call-and-response pattern. Blacks as well as whites attended camp meetings and naturally each group worked its influence on the other in the manner in which the religious songs were sung. Eventually out of this fusion there developed a new type of religious song which was called the "spiritual song" or just plain spiritual.

The spirituals, like "Go Down Moses" or "Ezekial Saw

the Wheel," that we hear today—indeed, which you may have sung—are only watered down versions of the original ones. As sung by slaves these were strong, dramatic, and heavily inflected with African rhythms.

Yet one more type of music created by blacks which was to have important effects was the so-called "shout" or "field holler." The field holler apparently performed no function other than to communicate the misery of one black to another. A slave, drudging endless hour after hour in a field, would suddenly straighten up and cast off a crying wail. One report from 1853 describes a field holler as "a long, loud musical shout, rising and falling, and breaking into falsetto, his voice ringing through the woods in the clear frosty night air, like a bugle call. As he finished, the melody was caught up by another, and then another, then by several in chorus." Unfortunately, we know less about field hollers than we do about other kinds of slave music; it seems clear, however, that field hollers were an important kind of musical expression for the plantation slaves, who made up the bulk of the blacks in the United States before the Civil War.

By the time of that terrible conflict, the black slaves in this country had developed out of African and European traditions a rich and varied body of music: work songs, spirituals, dance music, field hollers, street vendors' cries. Each of these different types of music had its own special meaning and own special function but, as far as we are able to tell today, they had in common two important features. One was the tendency for the performer to twist or bend certain notes away from what properly trained European musicians would consider "true" pitch. The second was a special rhythmic pulse which was somehow different from white music. During the 19th century a number of white writers made efforts to study, or at least report on, the music of the American blacks. They consistently found that the rhythms of this music were not easy to write down in standard European notation. Because there were no phonograph records in those days we cannot be sure exactly how those rhythms sounded, but it is certainly clear that the slaves had at least to some extent kept African rhythms in their music.

Thus, when the Civil War began in 1860, there existed among American blacks a highly developed musical tradition which was neither African nor European but something of its own.

The cataclysm of the Civil War tore apart the world that Southerners, both black and white, had known for generations. At its conclusion millions of slaves found themselves free—but free to do what? On the day of "jubilo" hundreds of thousands of them stood at plantation gates wondering where to go and what to do. Uneducated, mainly unskilled, they knew no way to make their livings except the one they had always known: working the fields. In time, unscrupulous whites, both Southern and Northern, began to take advantage of the ignorance of the black people. During the "reconstruction" period Southern law-makers began to pass the so-called "Jim Crow" laws which effectively put the blacks back into the bondage they had only recently escaped. Where law failed, terror tactics and lynchings did their work. Twenty years after the Civil War ended the black man was as well imprisoned by poverty, debt, and racial law as he had been by slavery. And somewhere during this period he began to create yet one more musical form, a form which is still with us today, essentially unchanged: the blues, on which jazz was eventually to be built.

I'll discuss the blues further in a later chapter but I will say a bit about it now. It is hard to know exactly what those early 19th century blues were like. It seems likely that they stemmed out of the field hollers and the work songs more than the church music of the blacks, but we can't be sure. The blues is essentially a vocal rather than instrumental music, consisting of a three-line stanza, in which the first two lines are usually repeated:

> I hate to see that evenin' sun go down,
> I hate to see that evenin' sun go down,
> Because it makes me feel I'm on my last go round.

But there is more to it than that. Not surprisingly, it is very much part of the call-and-response form—but in this case the response is not sung but played on an instrument. The instrument might be the singer's own guitar or piano, but it could be a trumpet, trombone, or something else played by a supporting musician. In fact, it might be a whole big band which plays the responses:

> I hate to see that evenin' sun go down,
> (instrumental response)
> I hate to see that evenin' sun go down,
> (instrumental response)
> Because it makes me feel, I'm on my last go round.
> (instrumental response)

Furthermore, blues musicians employed those odd rhythms and bent off-pitch notes which were characteristic of all black American music. They still do today; although we cannot be sure, it seems likely that the rough country blues singers of today are producing blues not much different from what was heard in the cafés and beer joints of the black South almost a hundred years ago.

There has always been some confusion as to whether the blues can be called jazz. Jazz musicians play the blues and they are likely to think of the blues as just one type of jazz, not much different from other types. Other people, especially blues singers, are likely to disagree: they tend to see the blues as a distinct form of its own. I don't think it is very important to answer that question. It is a little like asking whether the water is the river: it is and it isn't. In any case, it is abundantly clear that the blues were the basic foundation on which jazz was built.

To see how this happened we have to know a little bit about the social situation in the South, especially in New Orleans, during the post-Civil War period. And this brings us into another controversial point. For a long time jazz historians held that the music was invented in New Orleans and spread out from there. Within the past ten or twenty years, however, other historians have stated that jazz sprang up in a number of places more or less simultaneously. They point out that there was jazz being played very early in New York and especially in Kansas City, Texas, and the Southwest generally. On balance, however, there are good reasons for sticking with New Orleans as the fountainhead of jazz.

New Orleans was a city with a rich musical tradition. According to Eileen Southern, "In the early nineteenth century, New Orleans was undoubtedly the most musical city in the land. Sometimes as many as three opera companies were playing at the same time; there were plays and concerts and balls and street parades, and most stirring of all, the yearly celebrations of Carnival or Mardi Gras."

The music was extremely varied. At one time or another the city had belonged to the Spanish, the French, and, of course, the Americans. Of particular importance were street parades: it was almost impossible for the people of the city to celebrate any occasion, however minor, without a marching band. In the post-Civil War period the demand for musicians was so great that clubs and organizations would often sponsor blacks who were interested in music—buying them uniforms and instruments and providing them with instruction.

This brings us to another most important and interesting point. There had existed in New Orleans, virtually since its founding in the early 18th century, a group of people known as Creoles. The term is not very exact but it was applied to people of mixed blood—perhaps French, Indian, black, or some combination of the varieties of people who came and went in New Orleans. The Creoles spoke a language of their own, had their own myths and folklore, and their own ways of doing things. In a word, they had their own culture. Although they were often dark skinned, indeed even black, they were considered in New Orleans through most of the 18th and 19th centuries to be a kind of racial halfway house. They were not slaves —Creoles were mainly free—but on the other hand they were considered by the whites to be somewhat "inferior," and consequently could not normally expect to rise to the top politically, professionally, or socially.

New Orleans Creoles in turn considered themselves "above" the ordinary blacks who did most of the back-breaking labor in the South. Traditionally, they did not work on the docks or in the fields but ran small businesses or worked in crafts. They might be cigarmakers, for example, or cabinetmakers, or run the corner grocery store. And they had a very strong tradition of music. It was not black music they were interested in, however, but the European music of the whites. This was inevitable: because they considered themselves "above" the blacks, the Creoles disdained black music. Creole musicians studied opera and concert music and when they played in marching bands they played according to Western rules, eschewing bent notes and African-derived rhythms. Creole music was white music, and some Creoles were master musicians.

The segregation laws of the post-Civil War period generally confined New Orleans blacks to the "uptown" district. Creoles, however, could live anywhere. In 1894, however, the city passed a law which lumped Creoles racially with blacks. The Creoles were forced out of their homes into the uptown ghetto district. Of course, the Creoles resented this bitterly but there was nothing they could do about it. And so there quite rapidly began to take place the final amalgam of European and African music which within a very few years produced the music we now know as jazz.

What happened was that the black musicians learned how to manage the trumpets, trombones, snare drums, clarinets, tubas, and saxophones the Creoles had always played; and the Creoles began to learn the rhythms and bent notes of the black man's blues. And then, in 1898, purely by chance the army bands from the Spanish-American War disbanded in New Orleans, flooding the pawnshops of the city with musical instruments. During this same period, in the mid-1890s, the city of New Orleans passed legislation confining vice to a certain area called Storyville, after Joseph Story, the man whose idea it was. There was plenty of work for musicians in the cabarets and dance halls of Storyville, and this gave an added impetus to the rapidly flowering new music.

What was this early jazz like? It came basically in two types—not surprisingly, one more closely related to the Creole tradition, the other closer to the black tradition. The first was the marching bands which performed not only in street parades but in public ceremonies or outdoor dances and parties. These bands played a music that was a good deal like what you can hear at any Fourth of July parade or between halves at a football game. Mixed in with standard marches were spirituals, hymns, and other types of church music, some popular songs, arias, and other concert pieces. This music was not really improvised. The players customarily "embellished" their parts—that is, added little figures here and there—but basically they stuck to the parts they read or had memorized rather than make up whole new melodic lines.

The blues bands, on the other hand, usually played in dance halls and beer joints. The bands were likely to be smaller, and the music more often improvised. They also may have played the marches and spirituals the marching bands played but the blues was their basic diet.

There was, in this period, a third musical stream which had a considerable influence on jazz history. Ragtime, which flourished from about 1890 until about World War I, was a piano music, sometimes adapted for whole bands, in which complex right-hand figures were woven over a left-hand rhythmic bass. Ragtime was not improvised but worked out and usually written down. It was highly syncopated but it did not employ all the subtleties of jazz rhythm and is not really jazz. Nonetheless, it showed jazz musicians, especially piano players, a way to go.

As you can see, jazz is something that grew out of circumstances. In a way, much of it was accidental. Suppose there had not been all those second-hand band instruments around? Suppose New Orleans had not forced the Creoles into the black ghetto? Suppose, to go back even further, the United States at its founding had abolished slavery, as many of the founding fathers wanted to do? But what happened, happened, and by about 1900 these streams from Europe and Africa, from the churches, black and white, from the slave quarters, from the New Orleans opera houses, from the levees and docks, from the cotton fields, from the ragtime parlors, from the street parades, from the vice dens of Storyville, had run together to make that brilliant American music which today has spread itself across the entire face of the world.

John Coltrane, who began as a bop player, made a major impact on jazz with his explorations into "free" jazz. Behind him in this picture is his wife Alice, a jazz pianist in her own right, who has been carrying on Coltrane's musical ideas since his tragically early death. (PHOTO BY CHARLES STEWART)

schools and styles

OVER ITS SHORT HISTORY JAZZ HAS BEEN BLESSED—
and cursed—with an amazing multitude of styles. Curi-
ously enough, they have come along about every ten years,
as a new generation of musicians arrives to try out its own
musical ideas. These changes have been a blessing because
ever-shifting ways of playing have given jazz a great deal
of variety in its short life. But these styles have been a
problem, too, because they have bred unnecessary antagonism among musicians. Too often players or fans from
one school become bitterly scornful of a newer style, while
the new arrivals are equally scornful of the older players
for sticking to the old ways. These feelings are understandable: after all, anyone develops loyalties to the things
he likes, and if you prefer a certain style of jazz you are
likely to think it is the true jazz, the best kind. Naturally,
you will resent other styles which claim to be "better."

It is particularly true that fans of new styles are likely

to be arrogant toward the older ways of playing. In the United States we tend to think that "new is best." We don't want to be old-fashioned, we don't want to cling to the same things our fathers liked. So when a new style comes along people sometimes decide that it must be better because it is newer. There's a certain spurious logic to this way of thinking: if the new style is building on the old it must surely be better because it takes what is good and adds to that.

This idea sounds right in theory, but in practice it doesn't always work out. What happens is that sometimes a lot of what was good in the old style is thrown out, too. The cubist painters of the 20th century built on the work of the impressionist painters of the 19th century but no art critic would say that cubism is a "better" style than impressionism. Or, to stay with music, many composers built on the work of the great Baroque masters like Bach but no one would say that these later styles are "better" than the Baroque style.

The truth, of course, is that there is something to be said for all styles of jazz. Each has its values, each has its drawbacks. The newer styles are not better than the older; just newer. Furthermore, there is this point: the new styles don't drive the old ones out. They may become more popular with listeners and musicians alike, but the old styles continue to live. Every major jazz style can still be heard live in the United States today. All styles still are represented on records and sometimes the older styles sell better than the newer ones. Consider the so-called "swing style," which ruled the jazz "roost" from the early 1930s to the early 1940s. It drove out of fashion the older New Orleans style. In turn, it was driven out by bebop, or bop as it is normally termed; and finally bop was supplanted by cool jazz. Today all these styles are still being played—not as much as they were when each in turn was at its height, but enough to remind you that each is still alive and doing well.

One of the biggest problems in discussing the various jazz styles is that they are not always very clear cut. Jelly-Roll Morton's early bands for example, definitely played New Orleans style. But in the 1930s, when he realized that the New Orleans jazz was out of fashion, Morton tried to mold his groups a little more into the swing shape then in favor. He didn't really succeed but, as you might guess, his later bands can't be so easily categorized as his early one.

Moreover, you often find in one jazz band players from two or even more different schools. Coleman Hawkins, for instance, who was one of the pre-eminent swing players, played with many bop groups in that style's early days, even though his own style was not truly a bop style. Billy Butterfield has played with both Dixieland and swing bands. Zoot Sims, who is basically a bop player, has played in Benny Goodman's swing bands. Furthermore, players often change their styles. Dizzy Gillespie began as a swing trumpet player and then went on to become one of the founders of the bop school. John Coltrane began in the bop school but ended up playing free jazz. But if it is sometimes difficult to label the jazz schools exactly, there are certain very clear trends we can follow.

The first, and to some people still the greatest, of the jazz schools is called the New Orleans style. This was the style that developed out of the fusion of the blues with New Orleans parade band music. Even today a marching band utilizes only a limited number of instruments: trumpets, trombones, and clarinets because they are loud and carry well out-of-doors; drums and tubas to keep the beat. Stringed instruments generally play too softly to be played outdoors unless you have a large number of them and, of course, a piano is too heavy to be carried around.

Developing out of the marching band, the early New Orleans jazz bands came very quickly to settle on a basic instrumentation of one or two trumpets or cornets (there's hardly any difference between the two), a trombone and clarinet, and a rhythm section which included drums, tuba, and perhaps a banjo. Later, as the bands began to play more in nightclubs and cafés, a piano was sometimes added to the rhythm section. This became the classic New Orleans instrumentation.

March band music is of course quite varied but if you listen carefully you will find that most often the trumpets play a fairly straightforward and simple melody, the clarinets play trills and quick figures above, and the trombones fill the gaps between the trumpet phrases in the bottom. The New Orleans style followed this pattern: melody in the trumpet line, clarinet filligrees on top, trombone fills on the bottom, with the drums providing a steady beat underneath all. And, of course, it was played with black rhythmic patterns, rather than the stiff left-right-left-right of a marching band.

The New Orleans style was mostly ensemble—that is, there were relatively few solos, and the band played together most of the time. Often the musicians would have some of their parts memorized but much of what they played was improvised. This "collective improvisation" is one of the hallmarks of the New Orleans style. No other jazz style has managed so well the trick of allowing several instruments to improvise at once. Obviously, when several musicians are improvising at once they can't simply play anything they feel like; the music would become completely chaotic. You must have to have some system, some set framework. But one advantage the New Orleans bands have for collective improvisation is their instrumentation. Trumpet, clarinet, and trombone have very different sounds, so that the musical lines made by each do not all run together in confusion. To further insure that they don't, the clarinet is supposed to play fairly high, the trombone fairly low, and the trumpet stay in the middle.

New Orleans-style bands played a wide assortment of music—the blues, of course, spirituals and marches which have been adopted for jazz, and original compositions written especially for them. Generally speaking they stuck to middle tempos, neither terribly fast nor terribly slow.

The first New Orleans player we know anything about is a cornet player named Buddy Bolden, who worked as a barber during the day. Because he stopped playing before jazz was being recorded, we have no exact idea of how he played. However, according to a New Orleans musician named Bunk Johnson who played with him on occasion, Bolden had a powerful and dramatic sound which could be heard "for miles." Bolden was born in 1868 and was playing jazz around New Orleans during the 1890s. In 1906 he began to have mental troubles and in 1907 he was committed to the East Louisiana State Hospital, where he spent the rest of his life, dying there in 1931.

The musician who replaced Bolden as "King" of New Orleans jazz men was Freddie Keppard, a powerful and inventive cornet player. Like Bolden, we know less than we should about Keppard. It is reported that he used to play with a handkerchief over his playing hand so that nobody could copy his system of fingering. In fact, Keppard was so worried about people "stealing his stuff" that when Victor offered him a recording contract in 1916 he turned it down, fearful that other musicians would copy his ideas from the record. It is a shame, for had he signed the contract he would have become the first jazz musician to record. Instead the honor went to a white group called The Original Dixieland Jass Band. This group has perhaps been down-graded too much by jazz critics, but in any case it was not as important as Keppard's group. Later on, Keppard did record, but he was by then past his peak and so we will never truly know just how good this fine New Orleans pioneer was.

The New Orleans musician pioneer about whom we know the most is Joseph "King" Oliver. Oliver's Creole Jazz Band was the first black band to record frequently, and as a consequence it had a wide influence. Oliver, furthermore, was Louis Armstrong's musical "father," and through Armstrong his influence has reached out into all of jazz. Oliver's story, however, like Bolden's, had a sad ending. Born in 1885 in Louisiana, he studied trombone and cornet, and began playing in the early New Orleans jazz bands when he was about twenty. His talents were quickly recognized and he became much in demand. In 1918 he moved to Chicago, working with various bands there, and in 1920 he took over the leadership of one of them, renaming it the Creole Jazz Band. He gathered around himself some of the finest of all the New Orleans musicians of the time, including Louis Armstrong, and from 1923, when he began to record, until 1928, when he moved to New York, the King Oliver band reigned supreme. The key to Oliver's success as a maker of music lay in the formal order which he imposed on his band. People sometimes think of jazz as being wild and uncontrolled, with notes darting and dashing around at random. In truth, any kind of music you don't understand is likely to sound like this. Actually, all types of jazz are played according to certain rules. This was particularly true of the bands led by King Oliver. The musicians were not allowed to improvise anything they wanted, but had to play within certain limits—that is, they had to stick more or less closely to ideas and lines worked out in advance. Says Gunther Schuller, a musician and writer who has studied the Oliver bands carefully, "The glory of the Creole Jazz Band is that it sums up—in Oliver's somewhat personal terms, to be sure—all that went into the New Orleans way of making music: its joy, its complexity, its easy relaxed swing, as heady as a hot summer night in New Orleans, its lovely instrumental textures, and its discipline and logic."

Unfortunately, this "discipline and logic" was Oliver's undoing. By the late 1920s Oliver's protégé, Louis Armstrong, who had left the Creole Jazz Band in 1924, was creating a brand new style of jazz which would sweep the New Orleans style into at least temporary obscurity. Oliver insisted that the New Orleans style was the only true way of playing jazz and he went on playing it to ever-dwindling audiences. Then he began having trouble with his teeth, which made it impossible for him to play the cornet. The band disintegrated and Oliver ended up in Savannah, Georgia, where he died in obscurity in 1938.

But the New Orleans style Oliver played so well was to live a second life. Brushed into the scrap heap during the 1930s, it was not dead but merely biding its time. In the 1940s and 1950s there came a revival of interest in this original jazz style. Although this revival occurred in the United States, its real resurrection took place elsewhere in the world. Traditional jazz or "trad" as it is often called, is today probably the most widely heard of the jazz styles outside the United States. It is played in cafés and dance halls all across Europe from London to Leningrad. In Europe, for example, the records of the old time New Orleans clarinetist George Lewis, whom most American jazz enthusiasts have hardly heard of, sell by the thousands. In America, Oliver's records are listened to mainly by a relatively small coterie of New Orleans jazz fans. In Europe, and indeed in many other places in the world, he is still an important influence.

Moreover, the New Orleans style gave rise to two minor styles, which branched off from the main line of jazz's development. The first of these was the so-called "Chicago style," a product of a group of young people, mostly whites, who began listening to the New Orleans bands in Chicago during the 1920s. Attempting to imitate what they heard, they created a music which was brasher and less controlled than the original. The most important of these young white musicians were the clarinetists Benny Goodman and Frank Teschmaker, and most important of all, Bix Beiderbecke, who died in his early thirties. Beiderbecke was a cornetist who played with a clarion bell-like tone—somebody once said that his notes sounded as if they were being knocked off by hammers. A masterful improviser who was harmonically ahead of most of his fellows, he created in his solos some of the most beautiful melodic ideas in jazz.

But on the whole the Chicago style was something of a dead end. By the early '30s most of the players had either moved out of it into the new swing style or had evolved with it into a minor but still vital and popular style called Dixieland. The Dixieland style is based on the New Orleans style, with its collective improvisation of trumpet, clarinet, and trombone over a steady beat. Rhythmically it is much closer to the swing style I am about to discuss, and there are many more solos than the New Orleans style provided for. On the whole, Dixieland is too thoroughly set and organized to allow for much great invention but it can be a forceful and exciting music in the right hands. Many of the best Dixieland bands were made up of white musicians associated with guitarist Eddie Condon. Worth mentioning especially are the trombonist Jack Teagarden, who was a great individualistic stylist more than strictly a Dixieland player; cornetist Bobby Hackett, who has a pure tone and creates lovely melodic phrases after the manner of Beiderbecke; trumpeter "Wild Bill" Davison who makes up in force and verve what he lacks in invention; and clarinetist Pee Wee Russell, an original innovator possessing a colorful tone, who stands out as one of the finest of all jazz clarinetists of any school. Most of these musicians came out of the Chicago School.

Dixieland and Chicago styles basically were variations of the traditional New Orleans style, and like the New Orleans style are still widely played throughout the world today. As a matter of fact, Louis Armstrong was featured

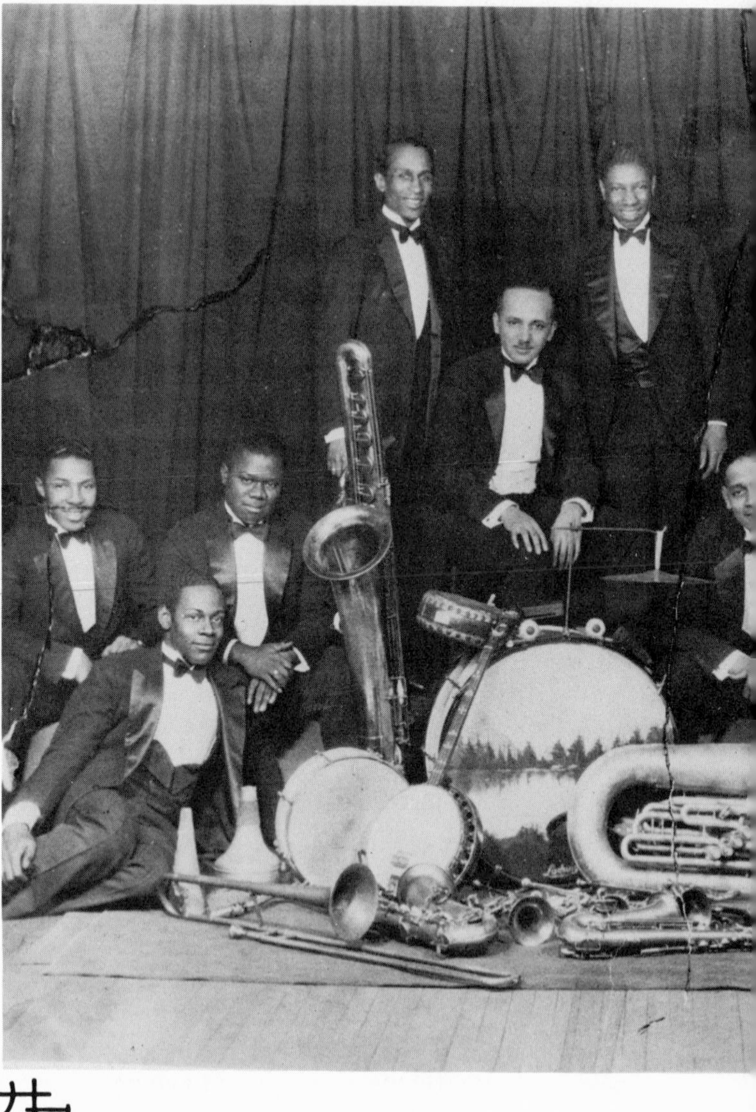

The Fletcher Henderson Orchestra in 1924. Louis Armstrong is third from left, next to the oversized saxophone. Coleman Hawkins sits on the floor in front of him. (CULVER PICTURES)

in a Dixieland band for the last twenty years of his life. But although these styles are still very much alive, they have stopped evolving and are still played today much as they were forty years ago.

The main line of jazz's development went in another direction. The style which replaced New Orleans jazz was the creation, almost single-handedly, of Louis Armstrong. People today remember Armstrong as a gravel-voiced singer of popular hits like "Hello Dolly," who also played a little trumpet. In fact, Louis Armstrong is generally conceded to have been the greatest jazz player who ever lived. Born on July 4th, 1900, he grew up in the New Orleans black ghetto surrounded by the new music which was still then in its formative phase. In 1914 he was sent to the Waif's Home in New Orleans, and here he learned to play the cornet. After his release he began playing around New Orleans and by 1922 his talent had become so obvious that King Oliver brought him to Chicago to play second cornet in the Creole Jazz Band. Here Armstrong learned to read and, after two years with the Oliver band, joined the Fletcher Henderson Orchestra, the forerunner of the big swing bands. He returned to Chicago in 1925 and there began, with various New Orleans-type groups, to make the records which changed the nature of jazz.

Armstrong's importance lies in the fact that he was an improviser of extraordinary inventiveness far beyond anyone else in jazz before him. A master of his instrument—the cornet and later the trumpet—it was obvious to everybody that he had to break out of the strict confines of the ensemble New Orleans style of the Oliver band. His head simply bulged with musical ideas which demanded expression and, inevitably, he began to work out a new way of playing jazz—the extended jazz solo.

The problem with being a genius, which Armstrong unquestionably was, is that nobody can really keep up with you. Armstrong simply had to be let to go his own way and, as his skills increased, the musicians he played with became more and more merely an accompanying cast whose main function was to weave a musical backdrop against which he could show off his skills. The first of the bands were the famous Hot Five and Hot Seven. These bands theoretically were playing the basic New Orleans style and, in fact, the very earliest did feature a reasonable amount of ensemble playing. But by 1928, when Armstrong was making some of his most enduring records, like "Tight Like This" and the classic "West End Blues" (according to some critics the greatest of all jazz performances), the band had become little more than a showcase for his triumphant solo playing.

The Hot Five and Hot Seven with which Armstrong made his reputation were only recording bands which never played together in public. During this period of the late 1920s Armstrong was playing primarily as featured soloist with various large bands. He was never really to be anything else again. After 1930 he starred with various large bands, usually organized by somebody else, in which virtually all the music was arranged to showcase his trumpet, which he was now playing instead of the cornet. To describe his playing is difficult. Certainly it was dramatic, sweeping, vibrant and warm. His influence over jazz musicians was tremendous. Not just trumpet players but everybody tried to work a little of the Armstrong magic into their playing. And of course the solo style took over.

But something else was happening to jazz, too: the approach to rhythm was changing in several ways. To begin with, the New Orleans bands tended to emphasize the first and third of the four beats in a measure. March music is always a "two-beat" music because people after all have only two feet to march with, and the influence of the marching bands continued to show in the more or less two-beat feel of New Orleans music. I say more or less, because the bands did not always emphasize just those first and third beats in a measure; nonetheless, there was a tendency for the music to have two major pulses and two minor ones in each measure. In the new swing style, the four beats in each measure tended to be played more equally, so that the music as a whole seemed to have a steady pulse.

In the second place, New Orleans musicians, in playing two quick notes together, tended to make the long one distinctly longer than the short one. If you understand music, the figure was played about like this: ♩‧♪

The swing players, in contrast, tended to play the notes a little more equally, something like this: ♪♪

And this shift also tended to smooth the music out a bit.

Finally, the tuba was dropped out of rhythm sections in favor of the string bass and the banjo was replaced by the guitar. String bass and guitar are lighter and sharper in their attack than tuba and banjo and again the effect was to give more evenness to the music. In general, then, jazz during the swing era began to be less "jerky," began to flow more smoothly over the measures.

A third factor in the creation of the new styles was the arrival of the so-called "big band" of twelve to twenty pieces, which played from written music. There had existed many types of large orchestras in the United States before: concert bands, symphony orchestras, pit bands playing in theatres, and of course dance bands. But because so few of the original New Orleans jazz musicians knew how to read music, there had never really been a big jazz band. The man who changed this was Fletcher Henderson, a pianist who had often accompanied blues singers on recordings. In time he began gathering together small groups for this purpose and by 1923, when the Creole Jazz Band was making its first recordings, he had a big band playing in New York City.

By the late '20s these three streams were beginning to come together: the solo style invented by Armstrong, the big jazz band pioneered by Henderson, and the subtle shift of rhythmic emphasis generally occurring everywhere. At their joining they produced a brand new kind of jazz which has been called swing.

The term is a bad one because it means three different things. In the first place there is that "swing feeling" so hard to describe, which is characteristic of all good jazz. Second, there are the "swing bands" by which term generally we mean the big dance bands of the 1930s and 1940s which sometimes but not always played with a jazz feeling. Finally, there is the "swing style" of the 1930s and early 1940s which I have just been describing. Confusing as the term is, we must nonetheless stick with it because it is the one in common use.

There were small swing bands as well as big ones but the big ones dominated. Most of the important jazz players of the era played in big bands most of the time, occasionally forming small bands to make records, or for a brief stint in a night club.

The Henderson band was the one which established the pattern for all the rest. In the very early 1920s Henderson was "house" pianist for Black Swan Records, the first black recording company. His job was to accompany singers on records and, if necessary, organize little bands to back them up. Almost by accident, in 1923 he got the opportunity to organize a band for the Club Alabam in New York. He began recording with this band not long after and for most of the next ten years his was always the most important of the big jazz bands.

Henderson's forte lay in picking out the best musicians and keeping them happy in his employ. At the beginning most of the arrangements were under the control of alto saxophonist Don Redman, whose role in the history of jazz has not been sufficiently appreciated. Whether it was Redman or Henderson who worked out the big band formula is not certain; probably credit must be given not only to them but to the members of the band itself who contributed their ideas. Essentially, the Henderson arrangements treated the band as three interacting sections: a brass section of perhaps three trumpets and two trombones; a reed section of four saxophones who also doubled on clarinet; and a rhythm section of piano, drums, tuba, and banjo—eventually replaced by bass and guitar. The rhythm section functioned much as it did in New Orleans style bands. Over this basic beat the reed and brass sections wove figures, sometimes one appearing alone, sometimes both together weaving in and out, sometimes answering back and forth in the call-and-response pattern. One crucial form was the "riff"—a simple figure repeated over and over. Often the brass and reed sections riffed against each other, perhaps one accompanying the other, perhaps in the call-and-response pattern. Mixed throughout were a great many solos. Because Henderson had so many great players over the years, the band was always able to offer one fine solo after another. On records these solos were short but in the dance halls across the country where the band played, a soloist might go on for several minutes if he was playing well.

The pattern established by the Henderson band became the standard one for the big swing bands which dominated both jazz and popular music from the mid-1930s until the close of World War II. Even today the pattern is heard in the few big jazz bands remaining—the Count Basie band, the Thad Jones-Mel Lewis band, and the one that is considered the greatest of them all, the Duke Ellington band.

Duke Ellington is one of the primal figures in jazz. Leonard Feather, author of the *Encyclopedia of Jazz*, once polled leading jazz critics on who were the most important figures in jazz. Duke Ellington was the only name on every list. Ellington is a fine jazz pianist and an excellent composer of songs but as he himself says, his real instrument is his orchestra, and it is this "instrument" which has made Ellington so important in jazz. Ellington, who was born in 1899 in Washington, D.C., began organizing small bands for dances and parties when he was still in his teens, but he didn't form the band which was to make his name until 1926. Gradually, over the succeeding years, he built the band up, carefully selecting men who were not only good musicians but who played with distinctive tones —such as Bubber Miley, who played a "growling" trumpet that gave the early Ellington band its so-called "jungle" sound. Later, the band included another growl trumpet player, Cootie Williams; trumpeter Rex Stewart, who got an unusual sound from his instrument by pushing the valves only partway down; a growl trombonist named "Tricky Sam" Nanton; Barney Bigard, a clarinetist with a fluid, rapid style; and alto saxophonist Johnny Hodges, possibly the greatest of Ellington's sidemen, who played with a tone like poured cream.

Working with this colorful pallet, Ellington began to create for his orchestra complete musical compositions which are more than just arrangements of songs. Although Ellington's brass and reed sections do sometimes play against each other, Ellington does not inevitably follow this standard pattern but mixes the instruments together in imaginative and constantly shifting patterns. He writes graceful and beautiful melodic lines, joining them together to produce unified wholes. But Ellington is not just a musical genius; he is also an excellent organizer and businessman. He has managed to keep his orchestra together for almost fifty years. It is not unusual for men to stay with the band for a decade or more; indeed, Harry Carney, Ellington's wonderful baritone saxophone player, has been with the band since 1926. One reason why the Ellington band is so superb is simply because the men have played together for so long.

The small swing bands echoed the solo style of the big bands. Usually consisting of piano, bass, drums, and sometimes guitar, plus an assortment of one to three horns, they were mostly vehicles for the soloist. There might be an arranged opening chorus, or more likely a simple statement of the melody, followed by several solos and con-

One of the qualities that made Duke Ellington so important in the history of jazz was his ability to surround himself with marvelous talents. One of these was Billy Strayhorn, at left, who scored many important works for Ellington. (CULVER PICTURES)

cluding with a repeat of the opening line. Casual groups put casually together for record dates, these small swing bands nonetheless made some of the most relaxed, easy swinging jazz on record. Often they were organized principally to showcase a famous soloist from one of the big bands, using musicians from that band to fill out. Count Basie's great tenor saxophonist, Lester Young, made many marvelous small group records, mainly with men from the Basie band. Various members of the Duke Ellington band, especially the alto saxophonist Johnny Hodges, similarly made records with fellow bandsmen. Bunny Berrigan, magnificent trumpet soloist with many swing bands, including his own, made some wonderful records with small groups. Indeed, for a time it became fashionable for the big swing band to have a small band-within-a-band which not only recorded but played occasional numbers at dances. Benny Goodman had a series of small groups which were almost as well-known as his big band. Bob Crosby had his Bobcats, Tommy Dorsey his Clambake Seven.

The man who started the big band movement, however, failed to reap its benefits. Easy-going Fletcher Henderson did not have the personality needed in the tough competitive struggle the swing band world became. By the mid-1930s, just as the swing craze was beginning to make bandleaders rich, his own band collapsed for good. In order to survive, he sold a lot of his best arrangements to Benny Goodman who went on to make them—and himself—famous.

The swing era lasted until just after World War II. The date of its death can be fixed precisely to December of 1946 when eight of the most important swing bands folded up. There were a number of causes for the disappearance of the swing bands but the main one was money. Club owners could no longer afford to pay the high prices these large bands needed to keep going. At various times leaders have attempted to put together new large jazz bands but few have lasted.

With the demise of swing a new style took over. In fact, the new style was already there attempting to shoulder the swing style aside. This new style was called bebop, or bop, and it proved to be one of the most controversial of all jazz styles.

The bop style was formed in numberless jam sessions, especially in the early 1940s, at Minton's, a Harlem night club, and Monroe's, an after-hours club also located in Harlem. A certain group of musicians who played regularly at these clubs were continuously experimenting with new sounds and new ways of playing. They included Charlie Christian, one of the first electric guitar players, who died tragically at twenty-four; pianists Thelonious Monk and Bud Powell; drummer Kenny Clarke; bassist Charlie Mingus; and trumpeter John "Dizzy" Gillespie. Gillespie, a very fine musician by any standard, was exceedingly important in founding the new music but the greatest of them was an alto saxophonist named Charlie Parker, known as Yardbird or simply Bird.

Parker was born in 1920 and died in 1955. With the exception of Armstrong and Ellington, no musician has had so great an influence as he did on jazz. True, other people, especially Dizzy Gillespie and Charlie Christian, made significant contributions to the creation of bop but so great was Parker's musicianship, and so magnificent his improvising skill, that he simply awed the musicians around him.

Parker was born in Kansas City and grew up there. He began playing the alto saxophone as a boy and became a professional musician as a teen-ager. He also, unfortunately, became a narcotics addict; drugs were to plague him the rest of his life and play a role in his early death. He came to New York in the late '30s with the Jay McShann band. He began playing around New York and thereafter his working life was somewhat chaotic, filled with brief stays of a few months with one band after another. More important is the fact that during the years around 1940 he was beginning to evolve the style that was to become bop. He has said that he began developing the sense that there were other ways to harmonize a jazz chorus than the ones then in use by the swing players. At first he could not figure out what it was he was sensing; but then one night, playing the song "Cherokee" in an unimportant New York night club, he suddenly found a new way of harmonizing the melody.

This story may not be exactly true but in any case, what Parker had grasped was a new theory of harmonies —new to jazz, although certainly not new to classical music—which involved playing what had been considered before "wrong" notes. Bop harmonies are more complicated than those used before. These "wrong" notes had been used for special effects but the bop players began playing them in wholesale lots. To many people the new music sounded harsh and discordant. Dizzy Gillespie had been working in the same direction as Parker. The two soon became musical partners and by 1945 young musicians everywhere were being attracted to the new style.

Bop was not only harmonically different from what preceded it but rhythmically different as well. The process begun by swing, of smoothing out the rhythmic flow in jazz, was carried further. In playing two short notes together the bop players tended to make them virtually equal. Their solos were likely to consist of long cascades of very fast notes. Again, swing players preferred medium tempos; bop players tended to work in either very fast or very slow tempos, although of course they used medium tempos, too.

Many musicians and jazz fans disliked this new music. Rhythmically and harmonically so different from what they were used to, sometimes they actually found it offensive. Some even called it "Chinese music." Of course some of the older players and listeners tried to understand what the new musicians were attempting to do; the great tenor saxophone player Coleman Hawkins was very sympathetic and encouraging to men like Gillespie. But for too many people bop was too difficult and it became a sore subject, a source of controversy and antagonism in jazz. Furthermore, because it was more difficult to understand than swing had been, it never really developed much of a popular following. For a period during the late 1940s, after World War II, it was featured in a little group of night clubs along New York's 52nd Street, which was known as "Swing Street" and in some bigger clubs around Times Square, especially one called "Birdland," after the famous Charlie Parker. But it was always to some extent an underground music.

Nonetheless, bop remains an important jazz style today, still very much alive. It is still played in clubs, still recorded. As a matter of fact, many of its founders, like Dizzy Gillespie and Thelonious Monk, both in their fifties, are still fine jazz players.

Although bop was to continue to live as an important music, a new style began growing out of it when it was still very young. In 1949 a very young trumpet player named Miles Davis, who had played with Charlie Parker, began to make records with a small group he had organized. Although there were many excellent jazz soloists in the group, it was primarily notable for the highly organized, tightly controlled arrangements it featured. The new style was founded on the bop rhythms and harmonies, although it extended them further. The primary difference between the bop style and the new one had mainly to do with its coloration, its emotional quality. Bop, however complex, was a hard-riding music dominated by strong-minded, highly inventive soloists. The new "cool" school, as it came to be called, was concerned with control, subtle harmonic shifts, tone colors, and attention paid to details of loudness, softness, and attack. Miles Davis, for example, often used a mute in his trumpet. The cool style was much more "symphonic" in its approach than bop was. It was an arranger's music, and in that respect it was really more similar to the old New Orleans jazz of King Oliver, with its easy swing, and more or less carefully worked out lines, than it was to the more dramatic, impulsive solo styles which came in between. What it lost in aggressive force, it gained in subtlety, color, and discipline.

Perhaps the most consistently successful of groups playing this style has been the Modern Jazz Quartet, under the leadership of a fine composer and pianist, John Lewis, who as it happens had an important influence on Miles Davis when he made those first "cool" records. The Modern Jazz Quartet consists of piano, vabraphone, drums, and bass. Its very instrumentation forces it to look for subtle

Count Basie is a fine pianist, but his real importance to jazz lies in the durability of his big band, which, next to Ellington's, has consistently produced the best big band jazz over the long haul. For forty years the Basie band has featured a formidable list of jazz's most important soloists. (CULVER PICTURES)

effects, rather than relying on a forceful soloist to provide spark and excitement.

Both the cool style and bop style are still very much with us but an even newer one came along during the early 1960s which today dominates jazz thinking. This is the so-called "new thing" or to use a better term, "free jazz." It is really too early to assess this music, which is still developing; we do not know where it is likely to go from here. But there are some interesting aspects. In the first place, in free jazz the systems of harmony on which jazz has been based—indeed, on which most Western music has been based—are discarded a good deal of the time. The player concerns himself with creating "sheets of sound" or melodic lines that sometimes seem to range randomly around from one key to the next. Free jazz musicians will often play notes deliberately out of tune. Rhythms, too, are free: drummers don't keep a steady beat, but play what they want like any other instrument. Soloists thus can play more or less in "free" time if they wish. The second point about free jazz is that it is the first style since New Orleans which has attempted to allow for collective improvisation—that is, the simultaneous improvising of two or more instruments. The idea in free jazz is not that the improvisers stick to some previously set rules but that they listen carefully to what each other is doing and try to invent music which will fit together.

A number of musicians have helped to develop free jazz but the two most important undoubtedly are Ornette Coleman, who worked out much free jazz by himself in the face of heavy scorn from other musicians, and the late John Coltrane—yet another jazz musician who died early —who, using Coleman's innovations and some of his own, has had an enormous influence not only on other jazz musicians but on rock musicians as well.

Analyzing jazz into this series of styles or schools is a useful thing to do because it helps us to organize jazz so we can grasp it a little better. The distinctions are quite real, too: the fact that so many swing musicians were angry about bop taking over, and the bop musicians' scorn for Ornette Coleman's innovations, show how meaningful they are to the people involved. But we shouldn't forget, either, that divisions of this kind, whether you are talking about jazz, painting, or cooking, are in a way artificial. You cannot neatly pigeon-hole musicians into one school or another. Players change their styles, play with musicians of other styles, influence people, and are influenced. Nor, as we have seen, do old styles disappear when the new arrives. All of the styles, major and minor, which have existed in the short life of jazz are still played and enjoyed today. The crucial thing to remember is that all are equally good and equally valid. Who is to say today which ones will be remembered most a hundred years from now?

Bessie Smith was not only the greatest of all blues singers, but had style and "star quality" as this picture, made in 1925, attests. (CULVER PICTURES)

the blues

THERE ARE STYLES OF JAZZ AND SCHOOLS OF JAZZ, but there is one style, one school, which lies at the very heart of the music. That is the blues. The blues is where jazz came from and it is where jazz goes back to from time to time to freshen itself. Buddy Bolden played the blues and so did Louis Armstrong when he was inventing the solo style; so did Charlie Parker when he was elaborating the bop concept, so did Ornette Coleman when he was working out the ideas he contributed to free jazz. No true jazz musician is ever very far away from the blues. Armstrong played on dozens of blues records backing up singers. Both Parker and Coleman began their careers playing in the so-called "rhythm and blues" bands, the forerunners of what today are generally called "soul" music groups. Thus, the blues and jazz are so closely intertwined that it is difficult to tell where one begins and the other leaves off. In fact, many musicians will simply say that the blues *are* jazz and leave it at that.

As the term is used by jazz musicians, a "blues" is a specific music form. Although there are eight- and sixteen-bar blues, normally the term means a twelve-bar segment repeated as many times as anyone cares. (A bar usually is four beats long; the ordinary blues is thus forty-eight beats in length.) It is built on a standard chord progression or some variation of it. For those who understand a little music the progression is this:

$$/I/I/I/I^7/IV/IV/I/I/V^7/V^7/I/I/$$

This means that in the key of C, for example, the first four bars would be based on C chords, the next two on F chords, the next two on C chords again, the next two on G seventh chords, and the final two on C chords. There are a number of different ways these chords can be varied but none of the variations generally used depart from this model very much.

If you don't understand music, it will help you to understand that a blues is a kind of song which has harmonies but not necessarily any melody. In other words, as far as the musician is concerned, when the leader says, "Let's play a blues in Bb," he need not have any specific melody in mind. The musicians understand what the harmonies are in a Bb blues, and they will improvise their melodies to fit.

There are, of course, plenty of blues which have melodies already set out to them. "St. Louis Blues" is one famous example. "Tin Roof Blues," one of the most commonly played of all blues, is another. There are hundreds more blues with melodies already to them. Furthermore there are hundreds of songs with the word "blues" in the title which are really not blues because they do not stick to this basic twelve bar pattern. "Beale Street Blues" is not really a blues, nor is "Blues My Naughty Sweetie Gave to Me," nor is George Gershwin's famous *Rhapsody in Blue.*

In a jazz musician's terms, then, the blues is a *form,* rather than a particular kind of *feeling.* A blues can be fast and happy just as easily as it can be slow and mournful, and it can be played on instruments alone, without any singer. But the original blues were undoubtedly all of the things the word suggests: they were mostly sung, with the instruments only an accompaniment for the voice, and they were mostly about misery: death, old age, poverty, hard work, and love gone wrong.

As I pointed out in an earlier chapter, it is difficult to know exactly where the blues came from, but surely it was out of some combination of field hollers, work songs, and the spirituals which had long been part of the Southern black man's tradition. It also seems clear that the blues was not strictly a New Orleans product, but was widespread through the South before the outbreak of jazz in the 1890s. Exactly what those early blues sounded like, however, we cannot know for sure. Probably they sounded more like a field holler than anything else. What is clear about the blues is that it was not originally built on that harmonic structure I talked about earlier. It is fair to guess that it originally was based on something much closer to African types of melodies, which were still being brought into this country by newly-arrived slaves well into the 19th century.

What leads us to this guess is the existence of the so-called "blue notes." The blue notes are, by the standards of European music, wrong: they are off-pitch. They are the notes which lie between the major and minor third and major and minor seventh of the scale. Anyone who plays a musical instrument can easily learn to play blue notes. In the key of C, using an ordinary C scale—that is, C, D, E, F, G, A, B, C, with no sharps or flats—the blue notes will be in between E and Eb and also between B and Bb. Wind instrument players get this effect by "lipping" the note up or down. A trombone player, of course, only has to hold his slide halfway between the proper notes. Guitar players bend notes by pulling the string a bit to the side. In fact, all jazz instrumentalists find ways of playing these "wrong" blue notes because they are so absolutely essential to both blues and jazz feeling. Only the unfortunate piano player has trouble finding these notes which lie in the cracks between the keys; he gets some of the effect by playing the notes on either side of the blue notes both at once—that is, using our example above, playing the E and Eb or B and Bb together. (Some jazz scholars think that there may be another blue note around the flatted fifth note of the scale—Gb in this example—but the other two are certainly the main ones.)

The blue note does not lie exactly halfway between the proper notes on either side but varies. Some people play it a little lower, some a little higher. Indeed, the same player may play it various ways in the same solo. In general, there is a tendency for the blue notes to slide around, giving them a slightly indeterminant feel.

It should be remembered that blue notes are not merely notes played out of tune. They are specific notes played out of tune in a specific way, and this suggests that there is a long musical tradition behind them. And indeed there is; suggestions of blue notes can be found in African music, although not as we know them in America. Thus, the blue note was created when the black man attempted to fit his African scales to the European scales he found in the United States. The blue note is neither African nor European: it is American, the result of a fusion of the other two in the musical heritage of the American black.

The early blues was strictly a vocal music with instrumental accompaniment. Or rather, the instrument was used to supply the response to the vocal call. The instrument, more often than not, was a stringed instrument like a banjo or guitar. Often it was homemade. The banjo, in fact, was probably developed by American blacks from an African stringed instrument. The reason blues players chose stringed instruments is obvious: you can't sing while you're playing the trumpet.

When the blues became instrumental is hard to say. The early trumpet player Bunk Johnson reports that he heard the blues played in the 1880s, and Buddy Bolden was playing blues on his cornet in the next decade. The blues thus were part of the jazz heritage, perhaps the most important part, before there was really any such thing as jazz.

But the vocal tradition remained. All through the South black blues singers, both male and female, were creating endless blues in beer parlors and dance halls. Many of these blues singers were members of traveling shows, often minstrel shows, which moved from theatre to theatre through the South entertaining blacks and sometimes whites. These shows, which featured dancers and comedians as well as singers, were immensely popular and helped to spread both the blues and jazz across the South.

Then, in 1920, a well-known black blues singer named Mamie Smith cut a song called "Crazy Blues." It had an immense success, selling some 7,500 copies a week for months. Suddenly the record companies, then part of a new industry, realized that there was an enormous untapped market among black people for records. Scouts from the record companies began scouring the theatres and dance halls of the South for new blues singers. Although some whites bought these blues records, they were mainly being made for blacks, especially those living in urban ghettos. Ever since the Civil War there had always been a trickle of blacks leaving the farms of the South for the factories of the North but during the period around World War I this trickle increased to a flood. City blacks, feeling displaced in an unfamiliar world, welcomed the familiar sound of the blues. Despite the fact that records cost seventy-five cents, a considerable sum in those days, American blacks were buying between five and six million records a year. It is no wonder that the record companies were anxious to find new blues singers to record.

Although a blues in the hands of a jazz master perhaps rises to the level of an art, the blues is essentially a folk music. Like any folk music it takes for its subjects the deepest concerns of the people who make it and listen to it. Blues were about leaving the farm for the factory, like this one by Blind Blake:

> I'm goin' to Detroit, get myself a good job,
> I'm goin' to Detroit, get myself a good job,
> Tried to stay around here with the starvation mob.

> I'm goin' to get me a job, up there in Mr. Ford's place,
> I'm goin' to get me a job, up there in Mr. Ford's place,
> Stop these eatless days from starin' me in the face.

Mr. Ford's place of course was the Ford Motor Company in Detroit, where many blacks went from the South to work. Blues were also about death—in the following case the death of a much-loved blues singer, Leroy Carr, who died at the age of thirty in mysterious circumstances. This lyric was by his friend, a blues singer named Bumble Bee Slim:

Now people, I'm gonna tell you, as long as I can,
Now people, I'm gonna tell you, as long as I can,
'Bout the death of Leroy Carr, well, he was my closest friend.

On one Sunday morning, just about nine o'clock,
On one Sunday morning, just about nine o'clock,
Death came an' struck him, an' he began to reel and rock.

He said, "Lawd have mercy, I'm in so much misery,"
He said, "Lawd have mercy, I'm in so much misery,
He's my friend, you all got to do what you can for me."

So on Monday mornin' just about the break of day,
So on Monday mornin' just about the break of day,
He began cryin' and he was passin' away.

I then called the doctor on the telephone,
I then called the doctor on the telephone,
When the doctor came Leroy was dead and gone.

For the wandering black worker, often coming into a new place where he had no friends, the blues was likely to be about being lonely:

Woke up this morning, feeling sad and blue,
Woke up this morning, feeling sad and blue,
Didn't have nobody to tell my troubles to.

And of course the blues is about love. Sometimes it's happy, witness this verse from Joe Turner's famous "Wee Baby Blues":

Although not essentially a blues singer, Billie Holiday's work is characterized by great poignancy, an outgrowth of the many tragedies in her life. (CULVER PICTURES)

Wee, wee baby, you sure look good to me,
Wee baby, you sure look good to me,
Come on over pretty mamma, and talk a little baby talk
   to me.

But more often it is sad. The following lyrics are from
Billie Holiday's "Fine and Mellow," to my mind one of
the greatest blues performances on record:

My man don't love me, treats me awful mean,
My man he don't love me, treats me awful mean,
He's the lowest man that I've ever seen.

Love will make you drink and gamble, make you stay out
   all night long,
Love will make you drink and gamble, make you stay out
   all night long,
Love will make you do things that you know is wrong.

Love is just like a faucet, it turns off and on,
Love is like a faucet, it turns off and on,
Sometimes when you think it's on baby, it has turned off
   and gone.

There are other subjects for the blues singers: poverty,
illness, wealth, liquor, luck, and an occasional tragic event
like flood, fire, or a train wreck. But inevitably the blues
deals with the deepest and most vital part of human life,
and this, certainly, explains its powerful appeal. For the
black man, who often felt helplessly trapped in a world
run by whites, a world which offered him no escape from
poverty and work, no way to find his own place in the
sun, often the only means of venting his frustrations was
the blues.

In any case, hundreds of blues singers were available to
provide this solace. Many of them labored in the obscurity
of backwoods beer joints but others went on to become

famous and sometimes even rich. Huddie Ledbetter, known as Leadbelly, made an international reputation for himself in the 1930s and 1940s when he was discovered by the folklorist Alan Lomax in a Southern jail charged with murder. "Ma" Rainey, Ida Cox, and Mamie Smith were among the best known of the blues recording artists of the 1920s. Bo Diddley, Muddy Waters, B.B. King, and a few others have become famous as a result of the revival of interest in the blues by such rock stars as the Beatles, who formed their style in part on that of the blues singers. But without question the most famous, and considered by many the greatest, of all blues singers was Bessie Smith, sometimes called The Empress of the Blues.

Bessie Smith was born in Chattanooga, Tennessee, in 1894, and grew up in extreme poverty. She was a teenager when Ma Rainey, possibly the greatest of blues singers before Bessie, passed through town with a traveling show called the Rabbit Foot Minstrels. Bessie joined the show and traveled with it through the South for several years, serving an important apprenticeship. Finally, in 1923, by now a fully matured woman, she was asked to record for Columbia. Her records were instantly successful with the black audience they were aimed at. In the first year they sold two million copies and Bessie Smith was suddenly famous.

For the next several years she made a series of records that are considered by jazz critics as being among the finest of all blues performances and, of course, some of the greatest jazz on record. Her accompanists on some of these sides include Louis Armstrong and Fletcher Henderson.

What made Bessie Smith so remarkable? According to musicologist Gunther Schuller, "It is a combination of elements: a remarkable ear for and control of intonation . . . an extreme sensitivity to word meaning and the sensory, almost physical, feeling of a word; and related to this, superb diction and what singers call projection. . . . But . . . her careful diction was never achieved at the expense of musical flow or swing. . . . Perhaps even more remarkable was her pitch control. She handled this with such ease and naturalness that one is apt to take it for granted. Bessie's fine microtonal shadings, the various 'flatnesses' with which she could color a pitch in relation to a particular word or vowel, the way she could move into the center of a pitch with a short, beautifully executed scoop or 'fall' out of it with a little moaning slide; or the way she could hit a note square in the middle—these are all part of a personal, masterful technique of great subtlety, despite the frequently boisterous mood or language."

Unfortunately, Bessie's story does not end as happily as it began. By the end of the 1920s Bessie was very nearly finished as a famous singer due, according to the *Encyclopedia of Jazz,* to "the changing public taste, drastic revisions in the type of material she was recording, and her own increasing addiction to alcohol." After 1930 she recorded only once. She continued to struggle on, singing when and where she could, but in 1937 she was killed in an automobile accident. According to one story, after the accident she was refused admission at one Southern hospital because of her color and bled to death while being transferred to another, but this story may be more legend than fact.

Although the vocal tradition of the blues continued in jazz, the blues was more and more taken over by the instrumentalists. Singing became merely one way of playing the blues. The blues became as much an instrumental music as a vocal one; it became, in fact, a form, a framework around which jazz musicians could improvise. To be sure, the vocal side of the blues has always remained in jazz but today the vocalist is likely to be seen as one soloist among many.

Perhaps more importantly, when the jazz musician took over the blues, he played them in the same way he played other tunes. The blues musicians in the older tradition, even today, do not often know how to read music, and are likely to be very limited technically in what they can play and sing. They don't always keep strict meter, either, but sometimes add or subtract a few beats here and there from the normal twelve bar form as it happens to suit them at the moment. The jazz player, on the other hand is accustomed to keeping strictly to the form; in fact, when a group of musicians are improvising together, the individual players can't drop out beats whenever they feel like it, without reducing the music to chaos. Furthermore, as jazz musicians grew more technically skilled they did not want to confine themselves to the blues way of playing.

But this does not mean that the blues feeling went out of jazz. On the contrary, it had always been part of jazz. The bends, the blue notes, have always been used in jazz, even on tunes which had nothing to do with the blues. And of course blues singing remained in the jazz repertory. It is nonetheless amazing how few truly great blues singers there have been in jazz over the years. Louis Armstrong was a marvelous blues singer, and so was the trombonist Jack Teagarden, one of the few whites ever to develop a reputation as a fine blues vocalist. Two other men,

Joe Turner and Jimmy Rushing, who sang with Count Basie's band for many years, are recognized as master blues "shouters."

But of all the jazz singers after Bessie Smith, the one generally considered the most moving was Billie Holiday. Billie was not essentially a blues singer—most of the songs she sang were innocuous popular ditties forced on her by the record companies, and it was these songs that made her famous. Nevertheless, she could be a marvelous blues singer when she wanted to be—witness her classic performance on "Fine and Mellow."

Billie, like so many other black jazz musicians, lived a life riddled with misery. She was born in Baltimore, Maryland, in 1915. Her father was Clarence Holiday, a guitar player who had worked with Fletcher Henderson. The family broke up and she and her mother moved to New York in 1929. Without the support of a husband, they were subjected to terrible poverty. The story goes that the fourteen-year-old Billie, seeking money, walked into a Harlem night club and asked to audition as a dancer. She was terrible and the club owner told her to quit dancing and stop wasting his time. But she was desperate for money and she pleaded for a job, any kind of a job. Finally the piano player took pity on her and asked her if she could sing. So she began singing, "Trav'lin' All Alone." In her autobiography, *Lady Sings the Blues,* she wrote, "The whole joint quieted down. If someone had dropped a pin it would have sounded like a bomb. When I finished, everybody was crying in their beer, and I picked thirty-eight bucks up off the floor."

Thereafter she very quickly became known to musicians. She made a record with a short-lived Benny Goodman band in 1933 when she was only eighteen, and then in 1935 began to make a series of records with a small band led by the pianist Teddy Wilson which catapulted her into national prominence. Perhaps catapulted is too strong a word. Billie Holiday never had the great fame of a Dinah Shore or a Dionne Warwick. Nonetheless, for a jazz singer she achieved great popularity and by the end of the 1930s was commanding high wages.

Unfortunately, her private life was not so successful. Personal troubles dogged her. Worse, she had been involved with drugs from her teen years, and her narcotics addiction not only marred her life but sometimes kept her from working, for at that time a person convicted of a drug offense was not allowed to work in a New York City night club. During her later years Billie continued to sing and record but the hard life she led increasingly hurt her voice. In 1959 she was taken to a hospital suffering from problems complicated by her use of drugs and alcohol, and within a few days she died. Apallingly, she was arrested on her deathbed for a narcotics offense.

Billie Holiday did not possess the coarse vitality of some of the earlier blues singers like Bessie Smith. Her voice was lighter and less powerful. Yet the subtlety of her phrasing, the way she bent her notes, and the emotional warmth of her tones make her not merely one of the greatest of jazz singers but one of the greatest jazz musicians of any kind.

Today there are not many blues singers left in jazz. The jazz styles which have come along in the past thirty years, such as bop or free jazz, simply don't lend themselves very well to blues singing. Nonetheless, the blues remains the crucial cornerstone of jazz. Modern players continue to play the blues all the time, and those blue notes and bent phrases are an integral part of the music.

Outside of the main stream of jazz, as something all its own, the tradition of the blues singer is stronger than ever. Through the interest of some of the famous rock musicians in the older music, the blues has become almost a popular music with a world-wide following. It is an astonishingly vital music. It was in on the birth of jazz and seventy years later it infused another musical form, rock, with its ability to move the emotions:

Charlie Christian died at twenty-four, but he is mainly responsible for making the amplified guitar the important instrument it is today. His musical ideas helped to shape the thinking of the early bop players. (THE NEW YORK PUBLIC LIBRARY, Astor, Lenox and Tilden Foundations)

the
jazz life

PEOPLE LIKE TO ROMANTICIZE ARTISTS. WE CREATE legends of wine and women around Beethoven. We make much out of the fact that the great painter Vincent Van Gogh cut off his ear to present to a woman. When a great poet like John Keats dies at an early age we say it is not tuberculosis that killed him but poverty and neglect.

Jazz musicians have been romanticized in the same way. We read about legendary jam sessions, prodigious drinking bouts, blues singers with great souls, the beautiful young women eager to attach themselves to jazz musicians. Our fancy is caught by the tragically early deaths of such jazz giants as Bix Beiderbecke, Charlie Christian, and Clifford Brown. Indeed, it sometimes seems that the best way for a jazz musician to become widely celebrated in stories and books is to die young, especially from drugs or alcohol.

Inevitably, the truth is different from the myths and

legends. Like men and women everywhere, jazz musicians have children, homes, mortgages, pets, and money worries. Jazz musicians walk their dogs around the block in the evening, wash the dishes, go sight-seeing with their families on vacation trips, and shop in supermarkets just like any other people. But the fact remains that although jazz players are people like the rest of us, with the usual worries and satisfactions, most of them do not live what you would call ordinary lives. The odd hours they work, the traveling they do, the irregularity of their incomes, makes it difficult for most jazz musicians to establish the kind of stable, orderly lives that the rest of us are generally accustomed to.

To some extent, of course, the same is true of any sort of musician—indeed, of anyone in the entertainment world. Actors sometimes go on the road for weeks at a time, television musicians on breakfast talk shows may start working at six o'clock in the morning, and nobody connected with the arts ever can count on a steady income. But of all of them, jazz musicians have it worst.

Part of this has to do with the nature of the music business itself. We like to think of a musician as being constantly caught up in creative excitement—Lester Young inventing brilliant chorus after chorus, Jimi Hendrix exciting a huge audience, Aaron Copland scribbling out pages of great music. In fact, most of the people in the world of music are most of the time performing very ordinary music on very prosaic occasions. The vast bulk of the music made in the United States today has little or nothing to do with great art. It is the sentimental tunes turned out by trios playing dances, weddings, and parties. It is the background music for films, radio, and television shows which is usually made up of bits and pieces taken from other sources. It is the music for soap and toothpaste commercials, the half-time music at football games, the piano solos in cocktail lounges. Only a very tiny fraction of the huge amount of music fed into the American air at any moment is jazz.

Consider, for example, New York. Out of the thousands of restaurants, bars, and night clubs in the city, probably not more than a dozen regularly hire top jazz musicians at reasonable salaries. There are more places that sometimes use jazz bands and even more that permit jazz musicians to come in and play, usually for drinks and a few dollars; but in New York, as in Chicago, Los Angeles, and other American cities, there simply is far too little work for far too many musicians.

With supply and demand so out of balance, even the most famous jazz players sometimes find themselves out of work. The end result is that players, celebrated and unsung, are forced to work odd hours and travel great distances to keep themselves busy. Duke Ellington, one of the most important figures in the history of jazz, a man whose influence on the whole shape of 20th century music has been profound, is even today required to tour the world constantly in order to find enough work to keep his band together. Ellington is over seventy, and as one of America's most important artists, he ought to be able to lead a more comfortable life. But such is the nature of the jazz business that unless he keeps traveling thousands upon thousands of miles a year, he will have to give up his band.

And yet Ellington is considered lucky by most jazz musicians. By far and away the majority are not working in jazz most of the time. They are either playing weddings and dances, or working in pit bands, or, if fortunate, getting high-paying advertising commercial work; or they are simply not working at all. In an excellent book about modern jazz musicians by A. B. Spellman called *Black Music: Four Lives* (it used to be called *Four Lives in the Bebop Business*), the author points out that Cecil Taylor, an important avant-garde jazz pianist, has averaged about two jazz jobs a year. To make a living he has worked as a delivery boy, a dishwasher, cook, and record salesman. Taylor's bass player told Spellman, "Trying to make a living playing with Cecil is absolutely unbelievable, because there is no economic advantage to playing music like that. It's completely unsalable in the nightclubs because of the fact that each composition lasts, or could last, an hour and a half. Bar owners aren't interested in this, because if there's one thing they hate to see it's a bunch of people sitting around open-mouthed with their brains absolutely paralyzed by the music, unable to call for the waiter. They want to sell drinks. But when Cecil's playing, people are likely to tell the waiter to shut up and be still."

The jazz musician's problem of finding work is not new. Joe Oliver, a critical figure in the history of jazz, wrote this letter to his sister not long before he died at the age of fifty-three:

Dear Sister:
I'm still out of work. Since the road house closed I haven't haven't hit a note. But I've got a lot to thank God for. Because I eat and sleep. Look like every time one door close the Good Lord open another. I've got to do my own cooking, as my landlady and daughter both work out. I

am doing pretty fair. But I much rather work and earn my own money. Soon as the weather can fit my clothes I know I can do better in New York.

Joe

Here was one of the most important men in the history of jazz unable to come to New York in winter to find work because he didn't have a warm overcoat. He died five months later.

Thus, in order to keep busy, the working jazz musician travels steadily across the country from city to city. Often today he makes an occasional swing through Europe and sometimes visits Asia and Africa as well. Travel always sounds exciting but under the conditions that most jazz musicians must endure, it is simply grueling.

Worst of all are the so-called "one-nighters"—tours which last weeks or even months with the band playing a single night in most towns, with perhaps a split week in the major cities. Billie Holiday, in her autobiography, described such a tour with the Basie band in the mid-1930s:

> We'd play a whole string of riffraff joints, rough Negro dance halls in the South where people were sneaking in corn whisky from across the tracks, and then boom in the middle of this grind we would be booked into some big white hotel. We didn't have the right uniforms, clothes, equipment—the cats in the band didn't even have the right horns they needed—we'd all be beat from traveling thousands of miles with no sleep, no rehearsal, and no preparation—and yet we'd be expected to be real great. . . . Living on the road with a band, nobody had time to sleep. . . . At night, as Lester [Young] used to say, we'd pull into a town, pay two to four bucks for a room, shave and take a long look at the bed, go play the gig, come back and look at the bed again, and then get on the bus.

Gene Cedric, a tenor saxophone player best known for his work with the great pianist Fats Waller, tells about one-nighters in a book called *Hear Me Talking to Ya,* by Nat Shapiro and Nat Hentoff:

> One-nighters were very rough. Many times there were halls with no windows and inside there were thousands of people shouting and fighting. And it was very rough when you had to go over mountains to make another town and you'd skid on ice. Man, there were some long hauls between states. Many times we'd get into town, check into a hotel, and we'd actually hear them planning how they were going to start the fights and shooting where we were going to play that night. There were some of those towns that had special prices [for food and hotel rooms] just for the bands that came through, that were touring. When they knew we were coming the prices would be higher by twice as much. Many times we'd get in earlier though, before they had a chance to change the signs.

Even today, in a world of jet airplanes, the jazzman's traveling schedule can be grueling. Red Norvo, an important vibraharpist, was scheduled to play at the Newport (Rhode Island) Jazz Festival in 1968. He was playing a job in Disneyland, three thousand miles away. At 2:30 in the morning, when the Disneyland job was over, he left for the Los Angeles airport, and took a plane which stopped at both Kansas City and St. Louis, before landing in New York. He still had to get to Newport but the weather was bad in New York and no commercial planes were taking off. Norvo then chartered a Piper Cub. The pilot told him, "If I can see the Newport airport, I'll land." He could see it, so they went in. Norvo grabbed a limousine at the airport and raced out to the Festival grounds.

In the 1930s it became a fad to call musicians "counts" or "dukes" or "kings" of jazz. As one of the most influential players in jazz history, Lester Young was called "the president" or "Prez." (PHOTO BY CHARLES STEWART)

He got there just in time to play, and went on without even knowing who he was going to be playing with.

But the worst aspect of one-nighters that had to be faced by black musicians was racial prejudice. Although the United States today is by no means free of racial discrimination, the situation was far worse in the 1920s and 1930s than it is now. At that time, especially in the South, black people could not use the same public drinking fountains as whites, had separate waiting rooms in train stations, were required to sit at the back of buses. As a general rule, they were not permitted to eat at restaurants frequented by whites or allowed to check into white hotels. In the North such rules were not usually spelled out and racial prejudice was not so bad but nevertheless it existed.

A black musician living at home in New York, Chicago, or any other big city could usually avoid racial problems by living in his own apartment and sticking to restaurants where he knew he was welcome. It was not pleasant, certainly, to know that you were being discriminated against but at least at home the black musician was able to find places to sleep and eat.

On the road, however, the situation was different. Most of the jobs were played in small towns where the musicians weren't known and, in turn, they didn't know where to find hotels and restaurants which accepted blacks. In many cases such places simply didn't exist. A band touring along a dusty Southern road might go a hundred miles before it found a café or even a grocery store where the musicians could get some food.

These problems were especially difficult for black musicians working in mainly white bands. Before the mid-1930s there were no such mixed bands playing in public, although black and white musicians sometimes recorded together. It wasn't that the white musicians were prejudiced against blacks—although of course many of them were: it was mainly that the people who owned the theatres and ballrooms where the musicians worked were afraid that their customers would object to the sight of blacks and whites sitting side by side on the bandstand.

But in the mid-1930s that began to change. The first important breakthrough was the formation of Benny Goodman's small swing groups, which included black musicians Teddy Wilson and Lionel Hampton. Thereafter, black men began to work in white bands, at first as star soloists, but eventually on an equal basis. And for each of these players, often the only black man among fifteen whites, life on the road was especially hard. Billie Holiday, for example, traveled for a time with the white Artie Shaw band. When the band stopped along the way at a diner or road-side restaurant for a lunch of sandwiches and drinks, she often was not allowed to go in with the rest of the band. Usually the other musicians would put up a fight and in the end she often was permitted in with the rest. But finally she simply decided it wasn't worth all the trouble: she'd rather have somebody bring her sandwich out to her so she could sit in the bus and eat her lunch in peace. Roy Eldridge, possibly the most important trumpet player of the swing period, got so tired of it all that he once decided he would no longer play with white bands. He told a reporter for *Downbeat:*

> We arrived in one town and the rest of the band checks in. I can't get into their hotel, so I keep my bags and start riding around looking for another place, where someone's supposed to have made a reservation for me. I get there

and move my bags in. . . . Then the clerk, when he sees that I'm the Mr. Eldridge the reservation was made for, suddenly discovers that one of their regular tenants just arrived and took the last available room. I lug the baggage back into the street and start looking around again. By the time that kind of thing has happened night after night it begins to work on my mind; I can't think right, can't play right. . . . Then it happened. One night the tension got so bad I flipped. I could feel it right up to my neck while I was playing *Rockin' Chair;* I started trembling, ran off the stand and threw up. They carried me to the doctor's. I had a hundred-and-five fever; my nerves were all shot. . . . Later on, when I was with Artie Shaw, I went to a place where we were supposed to play a dance and they wouldn't even let me in the place. "This is a white dance," they said and there was my name right outside, Roy "Little Jazz" Eldridge, and I told them who I was. When I finally did get in, I played that first set, trying to keep from crying. By the time I got through the set, the tears were rolling down my cheeks. I don't know how I made it. I went up to a dressing room and stood in a corner crying and saying to myself why the hell did I come out here again when I knew what would happen. Artie came in and he was real great. He made the guy apologize that he wouldn't let me in, and got him fired.

Yet for many jazzmen, the most troublesome part of the jazz life is neither travel nor racial discrimination: it is drugs and alcohol. Musicians sometimes like to claim that there are no more drug addicts or alcoholics among jazz musicians than there are among doctors or advertising executives. But although nobody has ever made a survey, the reality has to be faced: there are so many heavy drinkers and dope-users in jazz that drugs and alcohol almost have to be thought of as occupational hazards. I am not claiming that *all* musicians abuse themselves in these ways. A large percentage, probably the majority, use liquor and drugs moderately; many don't use either. But it is equally true to say that most jazz musicians at one time or another have experimented with both; and a very considerable percentage of them have ended up with a drink or drug habit.

In a way, the problems with liquor are understandable. Jazz is mostly played in night clubs, cabarets, and dance halls where people are drinking. A jazz musician works in an atmosphere drenched in alcohol. Liquor is always there—not just in the background but in the foreground as well. Then, too, there is the question of what to do during the breaks. Most bands play sets of, say, forty-five minutes to an hour and a half, with breaks, at most a half-hour long, in between. The break is really too short to permit the players to do anything or go anywhere. About all there is to do to kill fifteen or twenty minutes is to go to the bar or sit in the dressing room and have a drink. Some musicians have made efforts to get around this by bringing books to read or work to study during the breaks; but a night club is hardly a good atmosphere for study, and in any case, towards the end of the evening most players are too tired to concentrate very much.

Drugs are a different matter; it is hard to know exactly why drugs have been so deeply associated with jazz musicians but it goes all the way back to the beginnings. Where classical music has for at least a century been played in theatres and concert halls, often in an atmosphere of hushed reverence, jazz, from the beginning, has been part of "good times." In the early New Orleans days it was certainly associated with what used to be called vice. To be sure, even in those days a lot of jazz, perhaps the bulk of it, was played at perfectly ordinary dances, picnics, and parties; but much of it was played in houses of prostitution as well; and drugs were there in the background. Inevitably, some young jazz musicians picked up the habit.

I don't want to get into the debate over whether marijuana and other types of drugs are harmless or not. There is no doubt, however, that the hard drugs, like cocaine and heroin, are very dangerous indeed, and there are very few musicians today who claim that drugs—or drink for that matter—makes them play better. Charlie Parker, one of the greatest of all jazz players, is quoted this way in *Hear Me Talkin' to Ya:*

> Any musician who says he is playing better either on tea [marijuana], the needle [heroin], or when he is juiced [drunk], is a plain, straight liar. When I get too much to drink, I can't even finger well, let alone play decent ideas. And, in the days when I was on the stuff, I may have *thought* I was playing better, but listening to some of those records now, I know I wasn't.

Charlie Parker knew all about it: he died at the age of thirty-four, and when the police took his body to the morgue they reported his age as fifty-five. It is not fair to say that drugs alone killed Parker. People do die from overdoses but generally speaking it is not liquor or drugs that kill, it is the long-term abuse of the body that does the job. Drug addicts and alcoholics don't eat properly, they often don't get the right kind of sleep, and in general they fail to take proper care of themselves. In the end they are wide open to serious illness. Some of the greatest of all jazz players, including Bunny Berigan, Lester Young, Bix Beiderbecke, and Billie Holiday, as well as Parker, died basically from the abuse of drugs and alcohol.

I want to repeat, however, that most jazz musicians are no more involved with drugs and liquor than are ordinary citizens in other professions. They resent accusations that to be a jazz musician is to be a drunk or an addict. There is nothing in the jazz life that forces anybody to misuse alcohol or dope. Nonetheless, the young jazz musician today must recognize that he is going to come face to face with these problems and decide how he is going to deal with them.

I have been talking so much about the bad side of jazz that you may be wondering why anyone would go into it at all. But of course there is the good side and that is the music. The true jazz musician loves his work so much that he is willing to endure low incomes, bad working conditions, and neglect in order to play his own music. Benny Goodman once said, "When the band started, we didn't have any special ambition or goal, and we didn't know what it was exactly that made the band sound the way it did. But it was work, and detail—and arrangements. Why, do you know, when a new arrangement would come in, it would be an occasion. We couldn't wait to get started on it, and we'd work for three or four hours on it right away. . . . When we started the band, the only purpose we had was to play music, and Gene Krupa, Teddy, Hampton, Jess, Hymie, and the rest, they had a purpose. It was their life, it was important to them." Benny Goodman today is wealthy and doesn't have to work; but he still loves to play his music, and from time to time he puts together a new band just to be playing once again.

This strong feeling for jazz seems to hit people early in life. In fact, jazz players often accomplish great things when they are quite young. Charlie Christian was only twenty-four when he died of tuberculosis but he already had laid the foundations for what was to become bop. Louis Armstrong was making important records with King Oliver when he was twenty-three. Billie Holiday was only twenty when she started making the series of records with Teddy Wilson which was to make her famous. Bix Beiderbecke was a star at twenty, Sidney Bechet at seventeen.

One reason why so many jazz players have matured early is because they started learning early. In fact, it sometimes appears that they never really had to "learn" to play jazz; they just absorbed it through long exposure. The trumpet player Muggsy Spanier once said, "In summer the Pekin [a Chicago café] kept its windows open, so I'd sneak from home just about every night and sit outside on a curbstone listening to the music. . . . I would go down to the South Side and listen hour after hour to those two great trumpets, Joe King Oliver and Louis [Armstrong]. . . . It got so that I knew every phrase and intonation that they played, just from listening, so that, in spite of myself, I was doing the same things—as nearly as possible, of course. . . . It was a friendly, happy thing and I was completely steeped in their kind of music—which I've been playing ever since, because I love it."

One way the jazzman's love of his music comes out is through the jam session. Where the term comes from nobody is sure; it may be a play on words around the name of "Jelly Roll" Morton. A jam session, in any case, is an informal jazz get-together, where the musicians improvise on the blues and standard tunes that everyone knows. Sometimes jam sessions are put on for audiences but many times the only audience is the musicians themselves. A

There is a scarcity of pictures of the fabled cornetist Bix Beiderbecke, who died young, and largely unknown to the general public. This picture was taken in 1923 when Bix was twenty. (CULVER PICTURES)

jazz musician likes to be paid for playing; but he is bound to play anyway, paid or not. The musicians play solos in turn and a jam session can go on for hours. In the 1930s, one musician from Kansas City, which was famous for its jam sessions, reported that he left a session to go home and change his clothes. When he returned they were still playing the same tune.

Probably the most famous of all jam sessions was the one that took place nightly at a night club in Harlem called Minton's during the early 1940s. Musicians would go up to Minton's from their regular jobs in order to jam and it was here that Charlie Christian, Dizzy Gillespie, Charlie Parker, Thelonious Monk, and a handful of other musicians worked out the ideas that led to bop and modern jazz. The story goes that, in order to discourage poor players from sitting in, Parker and Gillespie worked out very complicated harmonies that the other players couldn't follow; these became the harmonic foundation of bop.

Actually, the story is only partly true. Parker, Gillespie, and the rest had already been experimenting with new harmonies anyway. But there is no doubt that the competitive element they displayed has always been a part of jazz. Younger players have always wanted to push the older, established ones aside; older players have always tried to put the young in their place; and the new man in town tries to make his mark by challenging the local star on his instrument.

Jazz battles of this sort are generally referred to as "cutting contests." They date back to the early New Orleans days when bands would try to outplay each other, partly as a matter of sheer pride but also because the band considered to be best would get the most jobs and have the biggest audiences. For example, Buddy Bolden used to play at a place called Johnson Park. According to the book *Jazzmen,* "A short distance from Johnson Park was Lincoln Park, where John Robichaux's Orchestra often played. Some nights, when the time came for Buddy Bolden to start, there wasn't anybody in Johnson Park. So Buddy, saying, 'It's time to call my chillun home,' stuck his horn through a hole in the fence and the people came rushing. Soon Lincoln Park was emptied."

Another type of jazz battle evolved out of the custom of parading bands around New Orleans in wagons to advertise dances or night clubs. Sometimes two such wagons would meet by accident or arrangement on the street, whereupon they would attempt to blow each other down. Once this happened to one of the most famous of the early New Orleans trumpet players, Buddy Petit. The challenging band caught Petit when he had had too much to drink and couldn't play very well, and they "cut" him easily. The next Sunday, the same band happened to come upon Petit again, apparently drunk this time, too. They pulled their wagon up to Petit's and got ready to play. While they were doing that a friend of Petit's sneaked around behind the wagon and chained the wheel to Petit's so that they couldn't get away. Then Petit, who had only been feigning drunkenness, jumped to his feet and beat the challengers in the contest.

Jazz battles mostly are carried out in a good spirit but nonetheless, when a musician's pride as well as his livelihood is involved, deep feelings sometimes come to the surface. Cecil Taylor, a very advanced piano player whose work is still not widely accepted, once had a job in a place in Brooklyn, New York. Another group, playing less advanced music, had been working there, and they did not like the idea of Cecil Taylor taking over the job, especially playing his advanced type of music which they couldn't play themselves. The owner of the club hired Cecil but the man actually in charge of the club was on the side of the other musicians. After the first set he simply fired Taylor. According to Taylor's drummer, Sonny Murray, in the book *Black Music: Four Lives:*

> Cecil was very hurt, very dragged. . . . I said, "Well dig it, Cecil, they've insulted you and me and the rest of the group so let's get our hats." Cecil said, "Sonny, please let's just finish it. . . ." I went back down on my drums [and] one of the manager's friends told me, "Man, I don't want to hear you play no more drums." I said, "Get out of here and leave me alone. . . ." Anyway, he pulled out a very large switchblade and said, "You see this?" I took my drum set and closed it up, it's about six pounds and a very strong steel, and I said, "Well you see this? Now I will bust your head wide open, brother."

The incident was smoothed over but hard feelings still existed and the next night somebody hit saxophonist Jackie McLean in the mouth because he sat in with the Taylor group.

But generally, competition among musicians is worked out in a less belligerent fashion. Sometimes it's even hard to tell who won a jazz battle; each player's fans are sure that their own man played the best.

One of the most famous of cutting contests is still debated. The central figure in it was Coleman Hawkins, the masterful jazz musician who almost single-handedly turned the saxophone into a jazz instrument. Hawk, as he was sometimes called, played with the Fletcher Henderson band during the 1920s and even into the 1930s, perfect-

One of the greatest of jazz virtuosos, Coleman Hawkins
played with great force and possessed an endless flow of
musical ideas. With him in this picture is Don Byas, an
under-appreciated saxophonist in the Hawkins mold. (CULVER
PICTURES)

ing his style. From nearly the beginning he was acknowledged the king of the saxophone. But then in 1934 Hawkins moved to Europe where there was less race prejudice than there was in the United States and where he could gain some of the respect he felt he deserved. Other saxophone players, especially Lester Young, Leon "Chu" Berry, Hershal Evans, and Ben Webster, began competing for his title.

Then, in 1939, with World War II about to break out, Hawkins returned to the United States. Naturally all the other saxophonists were intensely curious to find out whether Hawkins had improved or changed his style. They all felt that Hawkins would be surprised to see how much *they* had improved; perhaps the Hawk was no longer king.

Word went around that the saxophonists were going to gather at a certain night club. Hawkins showed up and sat in the back, just listening and saying nothing. One by one the other players took their turns at soloing. It went on for hours, with Hawkins still sitting quietly in the back. Then finally he came up on the stand and played, demonstrating a new, more fluid style that he had developed in Europe.

What happened then depends on which version of the story you read. According to some, Hawkins blew them all down. According to others, he didn't. In any case, a few months later he recorded "Body and Soul," which was an instant jazz classic and one of the few jazz records ever to become a popular best seller.

Thus, it is clear that no matter how difficult the jazz life is, the true jazz player is willing to endure it in order to play the kind of music he loves. Consider this story told by Red Norvo which occurred many years ago when jazz was still very much an underground music:

> We got a gig (job) to play in Bar Harbor [Maine]. . . . They'd never heard wild music like ours, and we didn't get paid because no one came back to hear us, and the only way we kept alive was with little gigs around Maine. We came back from one of them, and when we got home and looked in the back [of the truck the band traveled in] all the instruments were gone. We'd bounced them all out, so the next day we retraced the road and we'd find a saxophone in a ditch and a trumpet in a cornfield and a snare drum in the bushes. We survived on apple pies made from stolen apples, flounders and clambakes on the beach, with butter bummed from a farmer.

Red Norvo today is in his sixties, and despite it all, he is still playing jazz, because he loves the music.

Although John Coltrane was best known for the innovations of free jazz, Ornette Coleman had been working on these ideas in obscurity for years before they were publicized. Today he is experimenting with violin, trumpet and composition, as well as saxophone, his usual instrument. (PHOTO BY CHARLES STEWART)

7

jazz today

IT IS ALWAYS EASIER TO LOOK BACK OVER TIME AND
see what the trends were in the past than it is to make
guesses about the present. In 1944 it certainly seemed as if
the big swing bands would dominate the scene for years
to come but by 1946 the big band era was over. Similarly,
in 1928, the New Orleans style being played by countless
groups in nightclubs in the big cities seemed to be a per-
manent part of the culture. On looking back, though, we
can see that it was already being pushed aside by the solo
style Louis Armstrong was bringing to full flower.

The jazz world today is dominated by two players and
one ghost. The players are Miles Davis, still much admired
and emulated despite his long period of leadership in jazz,
and Ornette Coleman, generally considered the most important figure in the so-called "free jazz" movement. The
ghost is the memory of John Coltrane, whose innovations
are beginning to filter down through all sorts of contem-

porary music. Coltrane, in his turn, was influenced by Coleman. Although he already had a major reputation before Coleman began to record, he recognized that Coleman was playing in a new way and he made a study of Coleman's music.

It is difficult to describe any kind of music but it is especially difficult to describe free jazz; many of the innovations involve *not* doing things, rather than doing them. Until now most jazz playing adhered to certain basic ideas which have been common to music for centuries. It used more or less standard Western harmonies (although colored by the bent and blue notes taken from the black tradition), and it followed a regular rhythmic pattern. A song could be any length—forty-eight beats long for a blues, sixty-four beats for some popular tunes, double or even triple that for others. But no matter how long it was, it had a definite length. Harmonically, it was felt that only certain notes would go with other notes at a given place in the song. The theory of harmony is quite complicated and full of rules. These rules have always been bent or broken by musicians but still it is fair to say in general that jazz musicians, like any others, have always more or less followed these basic rules in composing or improvising.

The free jazz players have abandoned these rules. Their idea is that any note can be played with any other note. For example, almost the first rule of harmony is that two notes a half step apart—that is to say a black and white key next to each other on the piano—are extremely discordant and should only be used in combination with certain other notes; but free jazz players may play whole melodies a half step apart. Furthermore, free jazz players do not necessarily play to any special length. This means that the bass player and the drummer do not have to keep exact time but use their instruments to state melodies rather than to set the beat. Ornette Coleman himself says, "My music doesn't have any real time, no metric time. It has time, but not in the sense that you can time it. It's more like breathing, a natural, freer time. . . ." Of course the free jazz players don't always play free: sometimes they play in a more usual way but their basic way of playing is to break the rules.

But this doesn't mean that free jazz has no rules. The crucial point about it is that the players must listen very carefully to each other so that they can respond to what the others are doing. It is not just every man for himself, as it sometimes sounds to people who are not familiar with it; the players are listening to each other and trying to improvise a musical whole that will make sense.

The free style is the dominant one in jazz today but this hardly means that it is popular with the general public. It seems doubtful that, like most jazz, it will ever be widely popular. But there is another trend in music today which undoubtedly will gain a wider audience if it continues. That is the emergence of a type of music which has been called jazz-rock.

The jazz-rock movement is an interesting phenomenon because it comes from both sides of the fence. On the one hand, some jazz players have begun to bring certain characteristics of rock into jazz—partly, to be honest, for commercial reasons. Miles Davis, with a record called "Bitches Brew," has made an effort to incorporate rock ideas in his music. Another important jazz-rock group is Weather Report, which includes pianist Joe Zawinal, for many years with the Cannonball Adderley jazz group,

Miles Davis, probably the most influential of contemporary jazz players, characteristically uses understatement in his work. Behind him in this picture is Julian "Cannonball" Adderley, a forceful, highly-skilled technician in the Charlie Parker vein. (PHOTO BY CHARLES STEWART)

and Wayne Shorter, a jazz saxophonist who has worked with Miles Davis. These groups use a beat which approximates the standard rock beat. They also have gotten away from improvising against a chord progression but instead improvise, as rock players do, around a particular scale chosen in advance. These scales are known as modes and this type of playing is called modal. Modes have been part of music going back into the days of ancient Greece; for a long period during the Middle Ages they were the basis of Western music. Modes are still an important part of much music around the world, especially in India. Jazz players have experimented with modes from time to time since the 1950s but today, through the influence of rock, they are becoming an increasingly important part of jazz playing; and it is especially the jazz-rock groups who are turning to them.

The other side of the jazz-rock trend is provided by the rock players who have more and more been adding jazz characteristics to their music. Probably the best known of these groups are Blood, Sweat and Tears, and Chicago, but there is an English group called The Soft Machine that has pioneered in the jazz-rock field.

These groups are not all cut from the same mold: Blood, Sweat and Tears uses a brass section and saxophones working against the normal rock rhythm instruments, while The Soft Machine puts emphasis on keyboard instruments. Again, Blood, Sweat and Tears plays very simply and directly, whereas The Soft Machine is inclined toward complex harmonies and unusual effects. But generally speaking, these jazz-rock groups use rock beats coupled with some "jazz-type" playing in the melodic instruments. Blood, Sweat and Tears, for example, many times gives jazz rhythms to the brass section. The solos played by the horns owe more to jazz than they do to rock, although of course they are underlaid by a rock instead of a jazz beat.

Whether groups like these will continue to move further into jazz we can only guess. Possibly the two lines will move together, producing a music heavily indebted to both. Or perhaps both traditions will continue side-by-side, as jazz and the blues have done in the past. We will have to wait and find out.

In any case, jazz today remains a strong and viable music. A statement like this may surprise some of the many jazz musicians who have such a difficult time making a living, but it is true. Jazz has never really been a "popular" music. It has never attracted millions of fans with the money to make the musicians rich. Jazz players often resent the wealth and fame which is heaped on their creative inferiors, musicians who ride one gimmick to fame. Nevertheless, they have to face the fact that, like artists in other fields, they cannot expect great fame. But they can expect that their creations will *live*. The music of Joe Oliver and Jelly Roll Morton is alive today. It would surprise Oliver, although probably not the egotistical Morton, to know that their records are still in print and still selling in record shops all across the world. The Original Dixieland Jass Band's records have recently been reissued; there is a vast amount of Louis Armstrong available; and nearly forty years after Bessie Smith's death a major record company is going through the expensive process of reissuing every song she ever recorded. These records are all available due not to any sentimentality on the part of the record companies but because people are *listening* to the music. The popular music of the early part of this century is forgotten; but jazz is a tough and durable music, and continues to live on.

Every major city in the United States has its clubs and cabarets that feature jazz; there is always some jazz being played wherever you go. Furthermore, all styles are represented. In our biggest cities, like New York and Los Angeles, all styles are usually available for hearing most of the time, with free jazz and New Orleans style sometimes being played in clubs a few blocks apart. Jazz lives; and it lives because so many people care about it deeply. It will shift and change as it has always done but its power and beauty will continue to attract people for a long time to come. But even if jazz should disappear tomorrow, it will have left its mark on musical history. The records already made will remain to delight and astonish people for generations.

the records

WRITING AND READING ABOUT ANY KIND OF MUSIC IS always a bit frustrating, because you really have to hear the music to understand it. It is one thing to explain jazz rhythms; it is another to actually hear them. Obviously, then, anybody who is interested in learning about jazz simply has to listen to it; there is no substitute. And that means getting hold of records.

It is difficult to imagine what jazz would have been like had it come along before the record was invented. Probably it would have remained a kind of obscure and undeveloped folk music of the New Orleans area, of interest mainly to folklorists and musicologists. Although live jazz bands traveling out of New Orleans to other big American cities, especially Chicago and New York, did make an impact, records are the chief reason that jazz spread so rapidly across the face of the globe.

But there is another reason why jazz and records are so

The original Dixieland Jass Band, despite its name, is not considered to have been an original or great group; but because it made the first jazz record, which became a best seller, the band was extremely influential in the early years. (CULVER PICTURES)

closely intertwined: without records the older jazz simply would no longer exist. As an improvised music, jazz is as perishable as an echo, disappearing a moment after it is created. As a result jazz *is* records. For those of us who love this music, it is shocking to think that except for records we might never have heard Louis Armstrong play "West End Blues," might never have heard Bix Beiderbecke play at all.

The first known jazz record was "Dixie Jass Band One-Step" and "Livery Stable Blues," played by a band called the Original Dixieland Jass Band in 1917. The group was a New Orleans band made up of five white musicians, who had played a brief but sensational engagement at Reisenweber's restaurant in New York. Today the band is not considered to have been very good; there are some people who say that it is hardly representative of the true New Orleans style. In all fairness, a black jazz band, not white imitators, ought to have made the first jazz records; but as I mentioned earlier, Freddie Keppard, the great black New Orleans trumpet player, turned the opportunity down. This first record was a huge success, mainly for reasons that didn't have much to do with jazz. "Livery Stable Blues" featured a series of barnyard noises—a whinnying cornet, braying trombone, and crowing clarinet—and it was the novelty of this, as much as the frantic new rhythms, which sold the record. In any case, it became the first million-seller, and "jass" or jazz as it quickly came to be spelled, became a national word.

Because of the great success of the Original Dixieland Jass Band records, the record companies began searching

---

* Note that early spelling of the word jazz varied.

for similar material. In the next two or three years bands playing in the same manner, some of them hastily formed, began to record. As the market for jazz records expanded, the companies searched ever wider for new bands and players who might be popular. By the early 1920s all jazz musicians of any stature whatever were recording and the boom was on. Posterity has been very lucky; virtually every player, major or minor, in the history of jazz has been recorded sufficiently to give us a fair idea of his playing. During the 1920s and 1930s at least 25,000 records with some jazz content were made. The major players, with hardly any exceptions, have all recorded extensively. There are very, very few neglected jazz musicians who were insufficiently recorded or never recorded at all. As a matter of fact, the reverse is the case. There exists today an appalling heap of bad jazz records which have little esthetic quality and are of interest to historians only. Too often the recording companies knew nothing about jazz; if it had that "raggedy" sound it was good enough for them and they put it out as jazz. Because the public didn't know much about jazz either, often excruciatingly bad records were widely bought as "hot jazz."

During the 1920s, which was known as the "jazz age," there was a fad for jazz and the white public did buy jazz records, although frequently they ended up with popular dance music dressed up with a jazz solo or pseudojazz rhythms. In fact, most of the real jazz records were aimed at the black market. In the record industry these were called "race" records and were listed in a separate catalogue for the convenience of record shops which catered primarily to black people. Most of the great jazz of the 1920s and 1930s was cut originally not because record company executives wanted to preserve the genius of a Louis Armstrong or a Bessie Smith, but because there was a market among blacks for this sort of music. Few record company chiefs had any idea that they were making a real contribution to music history with these obscure "race" records, which they saw only as perishable commodities designed to fill an immediate need.

But even so, we would not today have a great many of the early jazz masterworks had it not been for another, more intelligent fad—hot record collecting. Beginning in the late 1920s, a handful of people, mostly young white college students, became interested in jazz. Because there were no Lp's, no reissue programs, no real concern on the part of the record companies about jazz music, the only way these young students could hear the jazz they loved was to search out secondhand copies. These were, remember, the old 78's, which are no longer made. They were extremely fragile: they shattered when dropped, warped easily in the heat, and were quickly worn out by the heavy tone arms and coarse needles in use at the time. These young record collectors were the only people who realized the true value of the records and they spent endless hours searching through pawnshops, secondhand stores, cellars, and attics, especially in the black ghettos, for those priceless jazz items mixed in with tons of ordinary commercial records. Making their job difficult was the offhand way the record industry was run. Dozens of companies were founded, made a few records, and then disappeared, either because they had been swallowed up by another company or had simply gone out of business. Some of the bigger companies operated under several names. Sometimes a record might be issued on more than one label. The record companies might put out one band's records under several names. For example, some records by Duke Ellington were issued as the Chick Winters Orchestra, Earl Jackson and his Musical Champions, The Traymore Orchestra, The Chicago Footwarmers, Lonnie Johnson's Harlem Footwarmers, The Whoopee Makers, Bunta's Storyville Jazz Band, Ten Black Birds, Ten Black Berries, Harlem Hot Chocolates, The Harlem Music Masters, Frank Brown and his Tooters, the Philadelphia Melodians, The Georgia Syncopaters, The Broadway Revellers, and even Louis Armstrong and his Original Washboard Beaters, although neither Armstrong nor any washboard was on the record. Conversely, some records by other people were issued as the Duke Ellington Orchestra.

This small handful of jazz record collectors not only saved thousands of irreplaceable jazz records from vanishing, but spent endless hours sorting out the confusion of names, labels, and players on the records. Of course some of the major record companies kept in their files the "masters" of the records they made but in thousands of cases the precious masters were lost as companies went in and out of business.

The heyday of jazz recording was the 1920s. By 1930, two things almost wiped out the record industry. One was the advent of radio, which brought not only music but other types of entertainment into the home and made the record player seem obsolete. The second was the Depression. As times went bad, beginning in 1930, dozens of record companies, small and large, collapsed, until by the end of the 1930s there were only three labels of any consequence left: Columbia, Victor, and Decca. These companies, fighting hard times, preferred to concentrate on what was commercially successful, which mainly meant dance music, popular vocalists, and the big swing bands, most of whom played little or no jazz. Many major jazz musicians gave up and got regular jobs. Sidney Bechet, the master of the soprano saxophone, worked as a tailor for some time during the 1930s. The only jazz figures who did more than occasional recording were people like Louis Armstrong who as a singer was an all-around entertainer and had a popular following. Most of the jazz that was recorded was made by a handful of obscure companies like Blue Note and Commodore, who were run by men who loved the music and were willing to run their companies for little profit.

Jazz record collectors suffered a second blow during World War II, when the government asked patriotic Americans to turn in their old records so that they could be melted down to make new ones. To their horror, record collectors saw millions of discs indiscriminately carted off in trucks for destruction. No doubt thousands of valuable jazz records thus disappeared. And yet again, from August 1942 to November 1944, because of a dispute between the musician's union and the record companies, many of the bands did not record at all. Thus, we have missed out on a moment in jazz history: Duke Ellington's band, for example, was at its peak during these years.

Then, in 1948, the long-playing record appeared. Its effect on jazz was immediate and important. Before the Lp, recorded jazz did not truly reflect the way the music was played live. In the night clubs, theatres, and dance halls, a jazz performance might easily last for ten or fifteen minutes depending on the number of soloists and how they happened to be feeling at the moment. It was nothing

for a fine soloist like the tenor saxophonist Lester Young
to improvise a dozen consecutive choruses on a blues and
there might be other solos in the same piece as well. Indeed, in an informal jam session, with many of players
wanting their chance to play, one number might go on
and on for a half an hour.

But the standard ten-inch 78 record could carry only
about three minutes or slightly more of music. (Although
symphonies were sometimes issued on twelve-inch records,
jazz virtually never was.) The short record meant that
everything had to be compressed. Solos were shortened to
a chorus or two, ensemble passages cut back.

The Lp changed all this. Now a piece could be recorded at any length the musicians wanted and we began
to get records that more truly reflected live performances.
At the same time, prosperity returned: people could afford
to buy records once again. Small companies began to crop
up everywhere, many of them devoted exclusively to jazz.
Once again, as in the 1920s, nearly everyone who could
play was being recorded and a great deal of bad jazz was
preserved for posterity. But surely that is better than neglect. After all, nobody is ever sure at the time which
musicians are going to seem important a generation later.
Better to record widely and let posterity sort out the chaff
from the wheat.

But the young person interested in finding out more
about jazz cannot wait for posterity. Which of all those
thousands upon thousands of jazz records are important?
How do you know which to listen to, anyway? Which
records are absolutely basic and belong in every jazz collection and which need only be listened to a few times?

The first answer, of course, is that you should listen to

Pee Wee Russell, at left, was a major figure in the Dixieland style, and is considered by some critics to be the finest of all jazz clarinetists. With him is Moe Asch, whose small "Folkways" company helped to keep important jazz in print. (CULVER PICTURES)

what you like. That goes without saying, but it is not all of the answer, either. Anyone who wants to understand jazz will have to pay attention to its whole scope and the truth is that it takes awhile for anyone to educate his ear to the point where he can understand and perhaps even enjoy all types of jazz. For the young listener, the early New Orleans bands are likely to sound incomprehensible; for the older jazz fan, free jazz may be difficult to understand. Thus, it is not merely a question of listening to what you like; there is also the idea of spending a bit of time trying to understand the types of jazz that don't really interest you.

The following list of essential jazz records is not simply my opinion but is based on the experience of many jazz critics and reviewers. None of them will entirely agree with this selection but most will agree with it in general. It is not a list of the "best" jazz records although it includes most of the great performers. Rather, I have put it together to give a clear view of how jazz changed and developed over the years from its beginnings in the 19th century.

I have tried primarily to choose records which are generally available. For this reason I have in some cases not chosen a player's best performances because I felt that some other of his records would be easier to find. Unfortunately, the term "generally available" is somewhat sticky. You can always find a performance of a Beethoven symphony in any record store; but this will not be true of any given jazz record, including the greatest ones. Few record stores will stock as many as half of the records on my list.

However, many libraries today, especially in our cities, have good record collections, and they will normally carry the majority of records on this list. Furthermore, serious jazz record collectors will own a good many of these records, as well as others no longer available which contain some of the same music. For example, in the mid-1950s there was an excellent mail-order reissue program on the now-defunct Jazztone label, which put out classic records by Billie Holiday, Lester Young, and many other swing stars, not always available now; some of these Jazztones may be in collections of a local jazz fan.

It is important to realize that all of the earlier records on this list are reissues. They were originally issued as 78 "singles." The Lp did not appear until 1948. Over the years most important jazz of those early days has been reissued on Lp at one time or another but many of those reissues have disappeared, too. What records are available at any given moment is a matter of chance. If the company which owns a certain record doesn't think it will make money on it, it won't put it out, although some record companies have made efforts to keep their important jazz records in print as a matter of conscience.

Furthermore, how a reissue is packaged and organized is a matter of record company whim. Sometimes a company will bundle together a group of older records in what seems to be an almost haphazard fashion. Other times, if they happen to have a few cuts they know will sell, they will reissue them along with a lot of inferior material to fill out the record. Nonetheless, at the present moment there is a considerable body of reissue material available. A jazz fan with some money to spend ought to make a point of buying some of the more important reissues while they are still in the stores.

I want to caution you that you will find many of the

records listed here disappointing at first listening. A record that I have called "a masterpiece" or "a classic" or "a brilliant example" of something or other is likely to sound to you like a lot of tinny thumping. Partly this is due to the poor quality of early recordings. In fact, recording techniques in the New Orleans period were so bad that the bass drum had to be left out because the heavy vibrations made the recording needle bounce around. But a more important reason for the "funny" sound of these older records is simply your unfamiliarity with the music. Frankly, I don't expect that many readers of this book will very quickly become enthusiastic about the earlier jazz styles. As a teenager I did not particularly enjoy listening to New Orleans music and I only came to grasp the beauty of Louis Armstrong's work when I was over twenty. But I suggest that you try to listen to the examples of the earlier jazz several times. Once you begin to understand the music a little, your enjoyment of later types of jazz will be increased. And, of course, anybody who is really interested in contemporary music of any kind ought to know something about the music which so influenced the modern sounds.

Here, then, are the records.

the roots of jazz

Jazz Vol. I—The South, FOLKWAYS RECORD FJ 2801
Folkways is a small company that specializes in early music of various kinds. Most of the cuts on this record were made during the 1930s. Of particular importance are "Ol' Hannah," a shout or holler, probably much like the early

field hollers of the 19th-century South; "Juliana Johnson," an axe-chopping work song sung by the famous black folk singer, Lead Belly; "Dry Bones," a recording made at a black church meeting; and "38 Slug," a prison blues song played by a band consisting of guitar, mandolin, washboard, and kazoo, which was typical of improvised bands of the black South in the 19th century. We cannot be positive that the 19th-century music jazz grew out of was exactly like that on the Folkways record but it is almost certainly very close to it.

Piano Rags by Scott Joplin, Vol. 1, Nonesuch H-71-248

There are several ragtime records available today but this one, played by Joshua Rifkin, who is a musicologist as well as an accomplished pianist, is especially good. Joplin is generally acknowledged to have been the greatest of ragtime composers. Later ragtime players often used breakneck tempos but Joplin preferred his music to be played slower, as Rifkin plays them on this record. Note that ragtime is not improvised, but carefully worked out—indeed, composed. Note, too, that it does not employ jazz rhythms, but seems somewhat stiff compared with the looser jazz swing. "Maple Leaf Rag," the first cut on this album, is the most famous of all rags.

the new orleans style

The Original Dixieland Jass Band, Victor LPV-547

Although critics no longer consider the ODJB, as it is universally known, a very good jazz band, it was enormously influential, in part simply because it was the first jazz band to record. Their first record, "Livery Stable Blues" and "Dixie Jass Band One-Step" was an instant best seller. For many years thereafter the popular idea of jazz was this kind of music. Young white musicians especially, who had little contact with the black world, took it for their model, at least until they learned more about black jazz. Many of the tunes on this record, like "Clarinet Marmalade," and "Tiger Rag" are still played constantly by Dixieland bands throughout the world. Probably the most important cuts to listen to on this record are the first three—"Livery Stable Blues" and "Dixie Jass Band One-Step" because they made up that first jazz record, and "Tiger Rag" because it was for a time the most popular of all jazz standards. Note that while improvised to an extent, the music is contained within a very tight framework. There are few extended solos but a considerable number of solo "breaks" in which one of the instruments has a brief passage to itself while the rest of the band halts. Note also that most of the tunes are arranged in three sections or "strains." If you are familiar with band music, you will know that most marches are also divided into three strains. The ODJB uses the same basic instrumentation as the marching band, too—cornet, clarinet, trombone, and drums, with a piano added. These devices make it clear how indebted New Orleans jazz was to the whole parade band concept. But despite its name, the Original Dixieland Jass Band was not original. Most of the tunes it played were versions of band numbers long in use in New Orleans and of course the players' whole idea of jazz was an imitation of the music of the blacks and Creoles of their home town.

Louis Armstrong: 1923, RIVERSIDE 12-122

Although this record was reissued under Armstrong's name, Armstrong was not the leader. This is really Joseph "King" Oliver's Creole Jazz Band. Oliver led a number of different bands through the 1920s and into the 1930s but this one is generally thought to have been his best. Certainly it was one of the most influential bands in the history of jazz. It was the first black band to record widely and both musicians and the knowledgeable jazz public considered it the finest jazz group of its time. Louis Armstrong, who played second cornet in the band, modeled himself on Oliver, at least at first. You will notice that the style of this band superficially resembles the ODJB in that the improvisation is confined within a tightly arranged framework. Oliver recorded some tunes two or three different times and even the breaks are similar or identical from record to record. Like the ODJB the Creole Jazz Band concentrated on ensembles rather than solos, with the solos often arranged as well, instead of improvised. But the similarities of the Oliver band to the ODJB are all on the surface; in its heart the Creole Jazz Band is vastly superior to the other group. Notice how the Oliver band gets an easy, rocking swing, as opposed to the thumpy rhythmic feel of the ODJB. Listen especially to the duet cornet breaks played by Oliver and Louis Armstrong, for example on "Southern Stomps." Again, in the ODJB the notes tend to come right in place in a four square fashion. In the Oliver records notes are bent, held out, or put in at unexpected places to give the music a true jazz feel. The ODJB learned to play jazz by listening to what the black players were doing; Oliver's musicians simply grew up with the blues. If you can't get hold of this record, there is *The Immortal King Oliver,* Milestone MLP 2006, which contains five Creole Jazz Band cuts, along with some of his later records.

The King of New Orleans Jazz: Jelly Roll Morton, Victor LPM-1649

Jelly Roll Morton was a fabulous personality who went around calling himself "the greatest" and claimed that he "invented" jazz. He didn't invent jazz, of course, but in fact he was very close to being a musical genius and could almost make good on his claims. A fine jazz singer, an excellent pianist and songwriter, his major claim to fame lies in the fact that he was the first true jazz "composer." Although prior to Morton King Oliver and others worked out frameworks for their jazz playing, Morton made actual compositions—although he did not necessarily write them down—for the musicians in his band to play. His band pieces were thoroughly organized, with the melody line shifting about from trumpet to clarinet trio to piano, with new melodies weaving in and out, with harmonies carefully arranged. To be sure, most of his pieces were partly improvised, but there are always very strong compositional elements present. This recording of Morton's "Red Hot Peppers" contains much of his finest work, as well as examples of both his piano playing and singing. Morton's flamboyant personality is evident throughout in the exuberance of the music.

The Louis Armstrong Story, Vols. 1-3, Columbia CL 851-853

If you had to pick the "most important" of all jazz records

it would undoubtedly be some of the cuts included on these three discs—Louis Armstrong's Hot Fives and Hot Sevens. Made between 1925 and 1928, these records capture the transition made by Armstrong from the New Orleans style of his predecessors to the solo style which continues to dominate jazz today. Cuts like "Cornet Chop Suey" and "Yes, I'm in the Barrel" recorded right at the beginning of the series, are essentially in the New Orleans idiom of Armstrong's idol, King Oliver. "Tight Like This," and "West End Blues" made almost three years later, are primarily display pieces for Armstrong's brilliant improvising. But these records are not merely of historic value: they contain some of the most expressive playing in all of recorded jazz. Every jazz fan has his own favorites among the Hot Fives and Hot Sevens but probably most would agree on "Struttin' with Some Barbecue," "Hotter Than That," "S.O.L. Blues," "Tight Like This," and "West End Blues" as being among the finest of the group. Indeed, Armstrong's "West End Blues" is considered by some jazz critics even today to be the single greatest jazz peformance on record.

The Louis Armstrong Story, VOL. 4

The final installment in the development of the solo style came in 1929 when Armstrong gathered around him a big band whose function was to act as a background for his trumpet playing. The occasional solos by other musicians in Armstrong bands thereafter were put in for a little variety and to give the leader a rest: Armstrong's own playing stood so high above anything else in jazz at the time that nobody could compete. He is here clearly playing in the swing style. This record contains a selection of some of Armstrong's best work with a big band. It includes two different "takes" of "Stardust" which indicate clearly how Armstrong varied his solos. But he made an enormous number of masterful records during the early 1930s, and there are other collections equally as good, especially *Louis Armstrong: Rare Items,* DECCA DL 9225, and *Louis Armstrong in the 30s,* VICTOR LPM-2322. There is also a whole series of Armstrong big band Lp's on the Epic label under the general title of V.S.O.P.

white chicago jazz

The Chicagoans, DECCA DL 79231

As I have said, the term "Chicago" jazz is something of a misnomer. Many of its players were from other parts of the country, and the style was played as much in New York as in Chicago. Nonetheless, the music played on this record has a distinct place of its own in the history of jazz. The young white Chicago players, mostly teenagers when they began, first became interested in jazz through the records of the ODJB and a white group called The New Orleans Rhythm Kings. Later they came under the influence of King Oliver and Louis Armstrong. In general, the music was less thought out, more often simply jammed, than the New Orleans music of Oliver or Morton. Hard-driving rhythmically, it sometimes lacks the easy swing that Oliver's groups achieved. Although there is much soloing, the New Orleans ensemble style predominates. Two other easily available records containing Chicago jazz are *The Golden Horn of Jack Teagarden,* DECCA DL 4540 and *Jack Teagarden,* VICTOR LPV-528. Teagarden himself, possibly the greatest of all jazz trombonists, was from Texas and not strictly a Chicago-style player but he did much more of his work with Chicago players associated with the style.

The Bix Beiderbecke Story, VOL. 2, *Bix and Tram,* COLUMBIA CL 845

Leon "Bix" Beiderbecke was unquestionably the greatest of the white Chicago players and one of the finest musicians in the history of jazz. A cornetist with a tone of marvelous clarity, he played with both precision and force, clipping off the notes, as somebody once said, like bells. As an improviser of fresh, expressive melodies he ranks with the greatest of jazz soloists. For much of his career Bix played with inferior musicians or was buried in the sections of the Goldkette and Whiteman big dance orchestras. These records were made mainly with pick-up bands put together expressly for recording purposes. They contain some of Bix's best solos, especially on "Way Down Yonder in New Orleans," "I'm Comin' Virginia," and "Singin' the Blues"—perhaps his finest solo. His piano work is exhibited on "Wringin' and Twistin'" and "For No Reason at All in C"; Bix was not a fine jazz pianist but his interest in advanced harmony is clearly shown in his piano playing. The "Tram" of these records is Frankie Trumbauer, an alto saxophonist. Trumbauer is not today considered a master jazz player but he was extremely influential in his time. These records were made in 1927 and 1928 and it is clear that the solo style initiated by Louis Armstrong a year or two earlier was already widespread in jazz.

the swing era:
the big bands

FLETCHER HENDERSON, *First Impressions,* VOL. 1,
DECCA DL 79227

As the major deviser of the big band style of jazz, Fletcher
Henderson's place in the history of jazz is secure. Henderson had important musical collaboration from Don Redman, his chief arranger, and other members of the orchestra, but the basic ideas appear to have been Henderson's.
On "Sugar Foot Stomp" notice the interplay of the sections, particularly in the first two choruses where brass
and reed alternately take the lead and supply background
figures. Notice also the clarinet trio, a Henderson trademark. "Just Blues," eloquent in its simplicity, employs the
call and response device, with soloists and even whole
sections of the band answering each other in turn. These
cuts also show to advantge Henderson's wealth of fine
soloists. They include, besides Coleman Hawkins and
Louis Armstrong, Jimmy Harrison, who laid the foundation for the swing trombone style; another fine trombonist, Benny Morton; Joe Smith, an inventive trumpet
player with a bell-like tone, who unhappily died early;
Tommy Ladnier, a trumpet player much influenced by
King Oliver; and clarinetists Russell Procope and Buster
Bailey, both of whom went on to have important careers
with Duke Ellington.

The Ellington Era, VOL. 1, COLUMBIA C3L 27

If Fletcher Henderson led the way with big band jazz,
the man who brought it furthest along the road was Duke

Ellington. Ellington is a piano player, but as he himself has said, his real instrument is his orchestra. His compositions have always been carefully tailored to the styles of the men in his orchestra, many of whom he picked for their colorful and distinctive tones, to give him a broad tonal pallet. Like Jelly Roll Morton before him, Ellington is not merely an arranger or songwriter—although he has written many wonderful tunes—but a composer of complete jazz pieces, usually employing several musical themes to make a unified whole. Ellington's genius consists in inventing expressive melodic phrases, organizing them into a solid structure, and coloring the result with the imaginative use of mutes and growls from the instrument at his disposal. This set of three records contains many of his finest cuts, including "Black and Tan Fantasy," "Mood Indigo," and "Sophisticated Lady" among others. *In A Mellotone, Duke Ellington and His Orchestra,* VICTOR LPM 1364, picks up where the set above leaves off. These cuts, made from 1940 to 1942, are generally considered the peak of Ellington's work, especially "Take the A Train" and "Cotton Tail," two masterpieces of big band jazz.

Benny Goodman Carnegie Hall Jazz Concert, VOLS. 1-3, COLUMBIA CL 814-816
Between 1935 and 1946 a hundred or more big swing bands recorded thousands upon thousands of records. Most of these bands played little or no jazz and even those which did mixed in a great deal of ordinary dance music with their jazz. Generally speaking the black bands played a little more jazz than the white bands but even a black orchestra like Jimmy Lunceford's, which contained some

Eddie Condon is not considered an important musician but he organized many of the Dixieland bands of the 1930s and 1940s. Here he is shown with singer Ella Fitzgerald, who has always been more of a popular than strictly jazz singer, and soprano saxophone master, Sidney Bechet.

fine jazz players, put out many records that can hardly be called jazz. Of the white bands, one of the best from the point of view of jazz was certainly Benny Goodman's. These records were recorded at one of the earliest jazz "concerts" and demonstrate how the band sounded in live performance. Goodman himself is a marvelous clarinetist and he always allowed a lot of solo space to the excellent improvisers he had in the band. Notice the riffs, the interplay of the sections, and the call-and-response of the Fletcher Henderson pattern. Rhythmically the band is a little stiff but Goodman was a perfectionist and you will not often hear such clean, accurate section work as in this band, especially by the trumpets.

Basie's Best, HARMONY HL 7229

Basie, who developed his first band in Kansas City, has been a durable figure in jazz—one of the few men to maintain a big swing band until the present day. Basie is a good jazz pianist, notable for a very spare style which employs few notes, but his importance to jazz is due to his band, which was, after Ellington, the best of the swing era big bands from a jazz standpoint. Like the Goodman band, it followed the general line laid down by Fletcher Henderson but what set it apart from other bands was the crisp, light swing its rhythm section produced and the high quality of its soloists. The Basie rhythm section has been famous since the 1930s; compare it to the relatively stiff rhythm playing of the Goodman band. No doubt this rhythm section was partly responsible for the eloquence of the soloists but they were also stars in their own right. During the band's heyday in the 1930s it included at the same time the great jazz master Lester Young on tenor saxophone; another fine tenor player, Herschel Evans; a preeminent trombonist, Dickie Wells; and a superior trumpet player, Buck Clayton.

Records of Basie's work in the late 1930s and early 1940s, when the band was in its heyday, are surprisingly hard to find. This record is representative but not necessarily "Basie's best." Another record available today is *Count Basie and his Orchestra,* UP FRONT 142. These are live performances and while the sound quality is spotty, there is excellent work by Lester Young and Basie's other soloists. Notice in both records "One O'Clock Jump," a Basie classic which demonstrates clearly the interplay of brass and saxophone sections.

small bands

Bechet of New Orleans, VICTOR LPV 510

During the 1930s an enormous number of small bands recorded a great deal of fine jazz. Many, if not most, of these were recording groups which did not play in clubs but were put together specifically by an acting leader to cut a few records. The bands were thus highly irregular, with the same musicians showing up over and over again with different groups. Although the many different styles were represented, these small swing bands had certain things in common. In general, there was little ensemble work, the main reliance being on solos strung out one after another. Usually the record opened with a fairly straightforward statement of the theme or an arranged riff. Then followed the solos and finally an improvised "jam" ending. Secondly, the rhythm sections, instead of accenting two of the beats in a four-beat measure, played all four with more or less equal emphasis to produce the gliding rhythmic feel which came to be called "swing." The cuts on this record are typical of the period. However, because Bechet and many of the musicians he played with grew up in the New Orleans style, there is more ensemble playing on these cuts than in most small bands of the time. Sidney Bechet was the greatest, and practically the only, master of the soprano saxophone until Coltrane took up the instrument in the 1960s. The instrument has a strong voice and Bechet's long, fluid, driving lines dominated most of the groups he played with.

Commodore Jazz Classics, MAINSTREAM 56003

An exception to the rule that small bands of the swing period did little ensemble playing is the so-called "Dixieland" style. Dixieland is a variation of the New Orleans style as it was filtered through the Chicago style. Most, but not all, of its players have been white. In its classic form, it follows the New Orleans tradition of the trumpet lead with the clarinet playing embellishments on top and the trombone filling the gaps below. However, there are more solos than was customary in the New Orleans band, there was a tendency to play faster and wilder than, say, a band like the Oliver band, and the rhythmic pulse was closer to the four-beat feeling typical of the swing period than to the older two-beat system. The cuts on this record are by a group of musicians associated with guitarist Eddie Condon. Condon is not considered a notable musician but he provided the organization and leadership for many of the best Dixieland groups. The driving Dixieland ensemble is heard to good advantage on this record, especially on "That's A Plenty" and "Royal Garden Blues," two

Dixieland standards. Prominent are "Wild" Bill Davison, a forceful if unimaginative cornetist, and Pee Wee Russell, a highly individualistic and expressive clarinetist considered by many the finest jazz musician on his instrument.

Signature, Classic Tenors, FLYING DUTCHMAN, FD 10146
Of all the players of this period, two of the finest were rival tenor saxophonists, Lester Young and Coleman Hawkins. Young made his reputation as star soloist with the Count Basie band. Hawkins started recording with the Fletcher Henderson band in the 1920s and was considered the king of the saxophone until the mid-'30s when newcomers like Young made their claims. This set contains some of their finest work. Notice especially the comparative lightness and ease with which the rhythm sections work. This smooth flowing beat allowed the soloists to "float" over the base they provide. Anybody who thinks that jazz is simple music should listen to the harmonic complexity and rich tonal texture of Hawkins' work on "The Man I Love." The Lester Young cuts also include excellent solos by trumpeter Bill Coleman and the highly-reputed trombonist Dickie Wells. Wells has a particularly fine solo on "Linger Awhile" in which he creates a powerful swinging feeling with a minimum of notes. These records are masterful examples of small band swing.

The Best of Django Reinhardt, CAPITOL TBO 10226
Though jazz is an American music, still it is surprising that there has only been one foreign jazz player of the very first rank. To be sure, there are today many excellent jazz players in other countries, but none of them would make a list of the top twenty-five jazz players—or perhaps

French Gypsy guitarist Django Reinhardt was the first and one of the very few non-Americans to become a major jazz figure. Most jazz guitar playing is still patterned on his work. Note the crippled fingers on his fretting hand, injured in a fire when Django was young. (THE NEW YORK PUBLIC LIBRARY, Astor, Lenox and Tilden Foundations)

even the top one hundred. The exception is the French gypsy guitarist, Django Reinhardt, a jazz musician of towering skills. Reinhardt did virtually all of his recording in France, often with visiting American jazz stars. He was a forceful rhythm player, who could swing a band by himself, but it was his ability to improvise long, fluid melodic lines that awed other players. With the possible exception of Charlie Christian, Reinhardt was the most influential guitar player in jazz and it is all the more a remarkable achievement when you realize that as an adolescent he was seriously burned in a fire and permanently lost the use of two fingers on his left hand. Also on these cuts can be heard Stéphane Grappelly, a violinist who was Django's major partner, and some American musicians Django often recorded with, especially trombonist Dickie Wells and trumpeter Bill Coleman.

the bebop era

Charlie Christian with Benny Goodman, COLUMBIA CL 652

The Benny Goodman Band never played bop but was firmly fixed in the swing idiom. However, the guitarist Charlie Christian, featured on these records with the Goodman band, was one of the formative spirits of the bop movement. His use of advanced chords, and his way of phrasing in long melodic lines across the natural structure of a tune strongly influenced the men who were beginning to create bop about the time these records were being made. Christian was not the first to use the electric guitar; but so influential was he that after his arrival to prominence the unamplified guitar virtually disappeared from jazz. Christian died at the age of twenty-four of tuberculosis after only two years of fame, but in that incredibly short time he left his mark on jazz. These records are fine examples of tightly controlled, well-organized swing. They include the excellent vibraphonist Lionel Hampton as well as Goodman himself. Goodman's small groups were extremely popular during the swing period.

Charlie Christian, ARCHIVE OF FOLK MUSIC, FS-219
These cuts were made on amateur recording equipment in 1941 in the Harlem night club called Minton's, where some young musicians met to jam. They included Dizzy Gillespie, Charlie Parker (who is not heard on these records), and Thelonious Monk, as well as Christian. Here they began to experiment with the new chord changes and the new approach to rhythm that were to become bop. It is interesting particularly to listen to Dizzy Gillespie, who had been previously primarily a swing band trumpet player. Here Gillespie is employing some of the new bop figures but at other moments he plays musical figures which could have come from the swing trumpet player Harry James. But already his technical mastery and enormous authority in the upper register is evident.

Dizzy Gillespie, VICTOR LPV-530
Gillespie, next to Charlie Parker, was the most influential figure in bop, and continues today as a master in that style. This record shows something of his development. On "King Porter Stomp," made before the bop period, he shows himself as a fine, if unexceptional swing trumpeter, highly influenced by Roy Eldridge, whose place he took in this band. (Eldridge, perhaps the best of the swing trumpet players, bridged the stylistic gap between Arm-

strong and Gillespie, just as Armstrong bridged the gap between the New Orleans style and the swing style.) Ten years later, when most of the cuts on this record were made, Gillespie was playing fully in the bop style.

The Essential Charlie Parker, VERVE V6-8409

There is available today a great deal of Charlie Parker material on records. Much of it is taken from tape recordings of concerts and radio broadcasts and is often poor Parker badly recorded. The cuts on this album were studio recordings made in the later part of Parker's career. His extraordinary command of his instrument and his astonishing flow of melodic ideas are evident throughout. His ability to dash headlong across the grain of a melody is clearly demonstrated in "I Didn't Know What Time It Was," despite the saccharine string accompaniment. "Kim" shows his skill at playing at extreme tempos while maintaining an easy swing. Unlike many great jazz players, such as Beiderbecke and Armstrong, who were often in inferior musical company, Parker was usually surrounded by fine players. Various of these cuts feature, among others, Dizzy Gillespie, Miles Davis, Thelonious Monk, John Lewis, and the two leading bop drummers of the time, Max Roach and Kenny Clarke.

Jazz at Massey Hall, FANTASY 86003

Undoubtedly the most important bop record, this recording was made at a concert at Massey Hall in Toronto. Its importance lies not only in its brilliant playing, but in the fact that it includes an all-star cast of the most important of the bop musicians. Besides Gillespie and Parker there is drummer Max Roach, pianist Bud Powell, and bassist Charlie Mingus, generally considered to be the best bop

The bassist Charlie Mingus has played with many major jazz figures. His importance to the music, however, lies in his influence on the younger musicians who have played with him. (PHOTO BY CHARLES STEWART)

players on their instruments and among the best of any kind of jazz players of any time or style. Note the tendency toward fast tempos and phrases built on long lines of fast eighth notes. Characteristically, the drummer Roach does not use the bass drum to keep a steady beat as jazz drummers had done before bop; he keeps basic time on the cymbal and uses the snare and bass drums for punctuation. Again, Powell does not keep a steady pulse on the piano, as earlier pianists generally did, but feeds the soloists with chordal punctuation. Notice also how much the right hand is emphasized in bop piano playing, with the left relatively neglected.

Blue Note Gems of Jazz, BLUE NOTE BST 82001

Much of the bop and cool jazz of the late 1940s and early 1950s was too different and complex to reach a wide audience. For the most part it was recorded by small companies with short lives. One of the most durable has been Blue Note, which from the 1930s onward recorded nothing but jazz. This sampler of material gives some indication of the musical ferment of the time. Notice especially the work of Clifford Brown, a brilliant trumpet player of whom much was expected but who tragically died in his twenties. Here he is featured on "Get Happy" and "Easy Living." Jay Jay Johnson, heard on "Get Happy" and "Tempus Fugit," was one of the leading bop musicians, a trombonist of extraordinary technical skills who set the pattern for trombone players for the next twenty years. Fats Navarro, yet another trumpet player who died early, played during his lifetime in the giant shadow cast by Dizzy Gillespie. Today his reputation is beginning to grow. Also on various cuts on this record are Miles Davis,

Thelonious Monk, Milt Jackson, and other important players of the time.

the cool style

Birth of the Cool, CAPITAL DT 1974

It is rare when a single recording session marks a milestone in jazz history. Not since the first of Louis Armstrong's Hot Five records did any single session have as much influence on jazz as did the earliest cuts on this record, which were issued as singles in 1949, for they founded the so-called "cool" movement in jazz. The cool sound was a reaction against bop, although Miles Davis, the most influential figure on these records, had been playing with Charlie Parker. As the name implies, the emphasis was on order and subtlety in tone coloration and harmonies. Unlike bop, where arrangements, in small bands at least, were often rudimentary and the emphasis was on "blowing" solos, the cool stylists worked within arrangements and sometimes complicated musical structures. On this record, Davis, who was to become one of the most important figures in modern jazz, already is demonstrating his penchant for simple, striking figures, and quiet, almost cautious sound in the medium range—a kind of musical modesty in contrast to his often strong personality. Although Davis is the dominant figure on this record, much of the new musical idea was worked out by arrangers Gil Evans and Gerry Mulligan, who also plays baritone saxophone on these cuts. Although these records made a great sensation among musicians, they were ignored by the general public.

The Genius of Gerry Mulligan, WORLD PACIFIC JAZZ
ST-20140
The early cool records of Miles Davis may not have captured much public interest, but many of the cool jazz groups which followed gathered a fairly wide public following. Particularly well known was the so-called "West Coast" sound. The partnership of baritone saxophonist Gerry Mulligan and trumpeter Chet Baker produced some classic examples of the cool style. Their first records, "Bernie's Tune" and "Lullaby of the Leaves," was a best seller in terms of jazz and made both men famous. Notice especially how Baker stays in the middle register, always playing with a quiet sound and careful attention to tone— a far cry from the bravura playing of Louis Armstrong or the explosive bop style of Gillespie. Notice also, as with the earlier Davis sides, the careful arrangements employing rich harmonies. Neither Mulligan nor Baker is considered a truly great jazz musician but their partnership was influential in spreading the cool style.

Milestones . . . Miles Davis, COLUMBIA CL 1193
Miles Davis has been a powerful influence in contemporary music, not merely in jazz, but in jazz-rock as well, for nearly twenty years—as much for his powerful personality as his musical ability. In contrast to the bop players, who ran high, fast, and often furious, Davis confines himself to the middle register and attempts to extract maximum value from a limited number of notes. Notice how he will work and rework one small musical phrase throughout a solo. Notice also how he places notes in odd and unexpected points ahead or behind the beat, undoubtedly due to the influence of Thelonious Monk. This tactic

is particularly apparent in the simple theme which opens and closes "Miles." Listen especially to how far he lags behind the beat in the "bridge" section (where the melody goes up) of the closing theme on this cut. (Also notice that the tempo drops just a shade as the tune goes on, showing that even the greatest musicians are not perfect.) This record also includes John Coltrane, when he was still playing relatively orthodox bop style, and alto saxophonist Cannonball Adderley, a hard-driving player whose work closely reflects that of his master, Charlie Parker.

The Modern Jazz Quartet, PRESTIGE PR 24005

The number of jazz groups which have hung together for more than a few years is very small indeed. The Modern Jazz Quartet has been in existence since 1952, and with the same personnel since 1955. The inspiring, driving force behind the MJQ, as it is universally known, is pianist John Lewis, who has tried to bring some of the techniques of classical music to jazz. A considerable part of the MJQ's music is carefully worked out in advance, often actually arranged, but the skill with which the improvised passages are woven in makes it sometimes difficult to tell which parts are arranged and which aren't. The other members are drummer Connie Kay, bassist Percy Heath, and vibraphonist Milt Jackson, a very hard-swinging and imaginative improviser who is considered the best jazz player in the group, and one of the best ever on his instrument. Notice especially how the music flows back and forth from one instrument to the other in much of the MJQ's playing. It is almost as if the players were holding a musical conversation with each other. Some of this interplay is worked out in advance, but much of it is improvised;

the musicians in the group have played together for so many years and know each other's styles so well that they can almost anticipate what the other is going to play.

Mingus Ah Um, Columbia CS 8171

Charlie Mingus is not very well known to the general public but he is one of the most respected figures in the world of modern jazz. Not only is he considered one of the finest bass players of the postswing period but his compositions have had an important influence on other players. Before Mingus, the bassist usually played straight harmonies on the beat to support the other players. Mingus, more than anyone else, turned the bass into a melodic instrument which played musical lines like any of the horns. He has played with half of the important names in jazz history, from Louis Armstrong to the latest modernists, and has always been interested in experimentation. He is known, like Jelly Roll Morton, Duke Ellington, and John Lewis of the Modern Jazz Quartet, as a composer of complete jazz pieces. Notice that "Goodbye Pork Pie Hat," written on the death of Lester Young (who was known for wearing pork pie hats), is not merely a basis for improvisation but a worked out composition. But Mingus, although an experimenter, has never forgotten his jazz roots. The first music he knew was church music and this influence is present in "Better Git It in Your Soul," which suggests the kind of singing heard at black churches.

Free Jazz

A Love Supreme, John Coltrane, Impulse S-77

John Coltrane, yet another jazz musician who died prematurely, is probably at the moment the most influential of the modern jazz musicians. An unknown saxophonist for years with various jazz groups, he gradually emerged as an important innovator, first with the bands of Miles Davis and Thelonious Monk, and then as a leader himself. During the process he broke further and further away from standard ways of playing jazz, abandoning the idea of improvising against an underlying chord progression, eschewing melodic phrases for sequences of very fast notes which produced "sheets of sound" and eventually making records, such as *Ascension*, IMPULSE A95, on which several players improvise at once in different directions. As you can hear on this record, there is no real melody in the traditional sense, nor anything like the ordinary musical organization of bars and choruses. Instead, over the course of improvising, Coltrane gradually expands and develops a few basic ideas. Coltrane's work is still controversial but his influence not only among jazz players but among the more advanced rock players is considerable.

The Shape of Jazz to Come, Ornette Coleman, ATLANTIC 1317

When Ornette Coleman first began developing the style which was to become free jazz, musicians accused him of playing out of tune and not knowing proper harmonies. Indeed, he was sometimes hooted from bandstands and even physically attacked for his way of playing. Today of course he is recognized as an important innovator and his method of playing is widely imitated. This record was his first and features trumpeter Don Cherry, for a long period Coleman's most important collaborator. Controversial when it first came out, today it seems rather mild in comparison with some of the things Coleman and other free jazz players are doing. Nevertheless, it is a landmark in the history of contemporary jazz, and listeners unfamiliar with free jazz may find Coleman's methods confusing. Notice particularly how the players depart not only from the structure of the song but from the beat itself. Note, too, the jarring harmonies and seemingly out-of-tune notes. Coleman believes that any sort of sound, regardless of orthodox theory, is permissible if it helps to express his feelings through the music.

piano players

Father of the Stride Piano, James P. Johnson, COLUM-BIA CL 1780

Jazz piano playing has always been a rather special art. For the jazz musician, the piano has the great advantage of being a complete "orchestra" by itself; but on the other hand it is difficult to bend notes or get great tonal variety. In general, the piano has been used in jazz bands mainly as part of the rhythm section, stating the beat and laying down chords for the other musicians to play against. Nonetheless, some of the finest of all jazz has been played on the solo piano. James P. Johnson is not the first of the great jazz pianists but he began early and had a great influence on pianists of his day. Johnson's work was based on the ragtime idea that the solo pianists must play as fully as possible, almost is if he were seated at a miniature orchestra. Johnson plays what is known as "stride" style: that is, his left hand seems to stride up and down the keyboard laying down the rhythm, while the right hand worked out melodic lines—as if the left hand were a jazz rhythm section and the right hand the improvising horns.

Blind musician Art Tatum is thought by many critics to have been the greatest of all jazz pianists. Although he occasionally recorded with bands, he worked mainly as a soloist. This picture was taken in 1941. (CULVER PICTURES)

The stride style remained the basic way of playing jazz piano until the bop period, when the "block chord" method came to favor.

Fats Waller, *Smashing Thirds,* Victor LPV-550

Fats Waller took James P. Johnson for his mentor but added an infectious, happy-go-lucky note of his own. Waller was a very popular entertainer who made hundreds of successful records. Most of them were of banal popular tunes picked for him by record company executives but Waller usually managed to turn them into good jazz by slyly kidding the tunes. He was a marvelous technician on his instrument and on this record he demonstrates his mastery of the stride style. There is probably no more joyous player in all of jazz than Waller, as you can judge by his own work on his own composition, "Honeysuckle Rose," but there was less joy in his life: Waller ate and drank too much, slept too little, and died at thirty-nine alone in a Pullman berth.

Art Tatum, *Solo Piano,* Capitol Jazz Classics, Vol. 3

Art Tatum, who was blind, is considered by critics and musicians alike to have been the greatest of all jazz pianists. He came out of the stride piano style of Johnson and Waller but, as he developed, his style grew more and more complex until the stride was buried under the mass of sound he tended to create. Indeed, some critics have said that Tatum sometimes let his playing get over complex at the expense of a true swing feeling. It is true that Tatum used a great many long runs down the length of the keyboard. But his extraordinary ability to invent new harmonies for a tune and his overpowering technique make up for his sometimes overflorid style and he can swing hard when he wants to, as witness "Somebody Loves Me."

Monk and Coltrane, RIVERSIDE 490

Thelonious Monk, like so many other jazz figures, was almost totally ignored by the public during the years he was making his first records. One of the formative figures in the bop movement, he eventually created an eccentric, angular way of playing which nonetheless has its roots in the stride style. Notice particularly on a tune like "Functional" his characteristic way of putting his notes in unexpected places ahead or behind the beat. Monk is also a marvelous composer of jazz songs; his "Round Midnight" is a jazz standard. The songs on this record are his own compositions. These records also feature the work of John Coltrane, who played with Monk for a period, when he was beginning his experiments with modern jazz. His "sheets of sound" style can be heard on "Nutty." Monk's influence on Coltrane, as on many other jazz musicians all the way back to the early bop days, has been profound.

The Story of the Blues, COLUMBIA G 30008

This excellent collection is taken from forty years of blues recordings put together by Paul Oliver, a blues authority. Whether the blues is jazz or not is a moot point, as I have said. Bessie Smith, Chippie Hill, Joe Turner, and his piano-playing partner Pete Johnson, all heard on this record, have long been considered jazz musicians. As this record clearly shows, however, there is a separate blues tradition which has continued side-by-side with jazz throughout its history. While jazz was born in considerable part out of the blues, today it is just as likely that jazz influences the blues as vice versa. Jazz rhythmic inflections are clearly evident in the blues but at the same time many of these players do not keep strictly in time and, in general, their improvising is limited. But what these blues players lack in musical skills, they make up in strength of feelings, and of course it is this simple, direct statement of emotion which has captured the attention of so many people in our complex world where we sometimes have trouble expressing ourselves.

Bessie Smith, The World's Greatest Blues Singer, COLUMBIA, GP 33

Columbia is currently in the process of reissuing all of Bessie Smith's records. This is the first one and includes "Down Hearted Blues," Bessie's first record, which was a best seller among blacks and made her famous. Bessie is considered by most jazz critics to be the greatest of all blues singers, not simply because she sang well but because of the intense feeling she brought to her music. Note how she slides through the notes, bending and twisting them to make her point. Bessie's singing demonstrates how the so-called "blue" notes are used in jazz. The first line of the song "Down Hearted Blues" is "Gee, but it's hard to love someone, when that someone don't love you." On the second "love"—the next to last word of the line—you can hear a perfect example of a blue note. Notice how Bessie seems to make a little scoop in the note, bending it away from its proper pitch.

Lady Day, COLUMBIA CL 637

Lady Day was the nickname of Billie Holiday. Billie was

not essentially a blues singer, although she did sing many blues, especially her classic, "Fine and Mellow." Most of her songs were popular tunes of the time picked for her by the record companies. Because of her fine musicianship she was able to turn this mediocre material into great jazz. Apparently it was impossible for Billie to sing anything without putting her own feeling into it; she would turn an ordinary love song into a profound personal statement. Billie did not live a happy personal life; her sorrows are clearly evident in her singing. Most of her early records, of which these cuts are examples, were made with small bands led by pianist Teddy Wilson, and included some of the greatest jazz players of the period. Both Lester Young and Benny Goodman accompany Billie on "I Must Have That Man," and Goodman, along with saxophonist Ben Webster and trumpeter Roy Eldridge, appears on one of her classic records, "What A Little Moonlight Can Do."

index